30 - 3

AFRICAN WRITERS SERIES

Editorial Adviser · Chinua Achebe

9 *Pat Amadu Maddy : Obasai and Other Plays*

Obasai
and Other Plays

PAT AMADU MADDY

HEINEMANN
LONDON · IBADAN · NAIROBI

Heinemann Educational Books Ltd
48 Charles Street, London W1X 8AH
P.M.B. 5205, Ibadan · P.O. BOX 25080, Nairobi
EDINBURGH   MELBOURNE   TORONTO   AUCKLAND
HONG KONG   SINGAPORE   KUALA LUMPUR   NEW DELHI

ISBN 0 435 90089 7

PR
9393.9
M 3
O 2

Printed in Great Britain by
Cox & Wyman Ltd
London, Fakenham and Reading

Contents

Obasai

CHARACTERS

BIG MISS B.K., *Mother of Majekudume and Wokhog*
MAJEKUDUME, *A tough bully*
WOKHOG, *School boy, Majekudume's brother*
ISAAC, *Brother of Ajayi and friend of Majekudume*
JOKUTOR, *Husband of Lagbaja*
LAGBAJA, *Village gossip and wife of Jokutor*
REV. J.J.T., *Village Pastor*
LOGAN, *Tenant of Big Miss B.K.*
AJAYI, *Isaac's sister, A common girl*
P.C. GBEP, *Policeman*
DADDY-JEBU, *Herbalist and trader*
A LAYABOUT
IST WOMAN
2ND WOMAN
CROWD, *mostly market women*

GLOSSARY

Egusi (*p. 4*) : pounded seed which is used as spice for cooking certain sauces.

Ja-gra-ja (*p. 6*) : difficult, hard times.

Gbada (*p. 9*) : nickname for policeman.

Chai (*p. 14*) : expression of disgust.

Jagae-butu-Jagae-tinap (*p. 21*) : consultation with a witchdoctor. Artifice used to explain the unknown.

Motically (*p. 26*) : bragging.

Kabor (*p. 31*) : welcome home.

DuDu Kam take (*p. 36*) : everything is there for DuDu to take.

DuDu (*p. 36*) : name of trawler.

OBASAI

Big Miss B.K.'s House: It is very early morning. The occasional bird sings from a distant tree. One or two dogs bark at intervals. In between the birds' singing and the dogs barking, from a fair distance, from every corner, the customary early morning salutation of Obasai village is heard off-stage.

VOICES: Hu-hu-huuuuuuuuuuuu.

VOICES: Huuuuuuuuuuuuuuuuu. (*As a refrain to the first voices.*)

VOICES: How are you-uuuuuuuuuuuu?

VOICES: We are all well-uuuuuuuuuuuuuuu.

VOICES: How is life-uuuuuuuuuuuuuuuu?

VOICES: Not bad-uuuuuuuuuuuuuuuu.

VOICES: How is home and family-uuuuuuuuuu?

VOICES: Can't complain-uuuuuuuuuuuuuuuuuu.

VOICES: What's happening today-uuuuuuuuuuuu?

VOICES: God alone knows-uuuuuuuuuuu.

VOICES: Let's look up to Him-uuuuuuuuuuu.

VOICES: He alone knows best-uuuuuuuuuuu.

VOICES: That's how it is-uuuuuuuuuuu.

VOICES: Let's hold on to Him-uuuuuuuuuuuuuu.

VOICES: Yes-uuuuuuuuuuuuuuuuuuuuuu. (*The voices fade away and are replaced by a gentle rather timid knocking on the door. Lagbaja calls quietly from outside.*)

LAGBAJA (*from outside*): Big Miss B.K.... Big Miss B.K. (*A slight pause. Footsteps walking on stones. A much stronger knock on window.*) Wokhog. Wokhog. Wake up Wokhog.

WOKHOG (*sleepily*): Eh? What?

LAGBAJA (*louder*): Wokhog, it's me 'L'. Open for me.

WOKHOG: Who is 'L'? Eh, 'L', who? (*Sound of door opening.*)

BIG MISS B.K. (*calls quietly*): Lagbaja is that you?

LAGBAJA (*tiptoes to front door*): Yes, Big Miss B.K. Sorry to wake you up so early.

BIG MISS B.K.: It's all right. Come in, Lagbaja. I heard the voice and thought it was you. But I wasn't sure.

LAGBAJA: You are quite right. I would have done the same. At such unsteady times like these we should never risk anything. You never know whether it is a thief, a killer or an evil spirit that will come imitating and impersonating your friend, neighbour or relative only to get at you.

BIG MISS B.K.: We have to be very, very careful. (*Town clock strikes six.*)

LAGBAJA: Funny, it is already six o'clock, yet all the house-wives and Saturday workers in Obasai are still asleep.

BIG MISS B.K.: How for do... they are tired.

LAGBAJA: I didn't know Wokhog was such a hypnotized sleeper.

BIG MISS B.K.: Like death. He sleeps like a wizard who goes on a witchhunt.

LAGBAJA (*chuckles*): Big Miss B.K. you never talk anything serious. Always too funny for words.

BIG MISS B.K.: But it's true. I tell you. Thieves can come into this house, take as much as they want. They can even take Wokhog from his bed, take his bedspread and pillows. He wouldn't know. He wouldn't as much as shake.

LAGBAJA: He beats records . . . (*Big Miss B.K. yawns. The church bell begins to ring from a distance.*) Big Miss B.K., I am going to the market, so I thought I should call and ask whether there's anything you might want, like ox-heel, trotters, tripe, fresh tomatoes, pepper or greens.

BIG MISS B.K.: As a matter of fact I do need some egusi and lettuce. (*Church bell stops ringing.*)

LAGBAJA (*enticingly*): I thought, knowing that Mr Logan is due home today, you might need some help also. Knowing that people will be coming and going out of the house at all times.

BIG MISS B.K.: You can say that again, Lagbaja.

LAGBAJA: I know our Obasai people. They will come to eat and drink and find out what you have to give them,

But they will never offer to even help carry an empty dish.

BIG MISS B.K.: Telling me? Our people like nothing but... free... I wonder where I left my purse last night.

LAGBAJA: In this Obasai, what I have noticed is, that if you allow them to know that you are a kind and sympathetic person, they'll want to ride you like a fool, turn you into a free prostitute and leave your house full of bastard children.

BIG MISS B.K.: You should never let them use your eyes to sleep. Never.

LAGBAJA: Did you find the purse?

BIG MISS B.K.: Yes. It was under my pillow.

LAGBAJA: Are we having a welcome home 'Awujor' for Mr Logan, Big Miss B.K.?

BIG MISS B.K.: I don't know yet. I suppose we might. But you know Revren' J.J.T. will be the first to call here when Logan arrives, and you know how it is like when those two are together.

LAGBAJA: At least we must pour libation and thank God and the dead ancestors for bringing him home again.

BIG MISS B.K.: Safe and sound. (*Changing the subject.*) Here, Lagbaja, do buy me two shillings and ninepence worth of lettuce and eightpence egusi. If you happen to see anything you think I might need...

LAGBAJA: I'll buy for you, especially if the prices are very reasonable ... It is in fact the reason why I am going so early. To meet good bargain... (*The alarm clock goes off.*)

BIG MISS B.K. (*shouts*): Wokhog! Wokhog!

WOKHOG (*from inside one of the rooms*): Eh! Yes, Mother. You call.

BIG MISS B.K.: Turn off that alarm clock. Don't you know it's past six o'clock? What are you still doing in bed?

WOKHOG: I am not sleeping, Mother.

LAGBAJA: Oh, yes! Children of this generation... May the Lord have mercy on them. Laziness is their will and pride.

Look at that my own Titty-Shine-Shine there at home. She is a woman the way she carries herself about. The best thing you can get her to do with a smile is to eat and go out parading half naked in that stupid thing they call mini-maximum.

BIG MISS B.K.: It's the same Lagbaja. They are all the same – three shillings and tenpence farthing. No difference whatsoever. You might say, yours is more beautiful than mine. But you can't say that yours is better.

LAGBAJA: That's exactly how I feel... exactly. (*Rising.*) Well, Big Miss B.K., I must be on my way.

BIG MISS B.K.: Good luck, Lagbaja. Good bargaining. See you when you return and hope you will give me some assistance today because I cannot rely on Wokhog.

LAGBAJA: Count on me, Big Miss B.K., I have already offered myself. So you can count on me.

BIG MISS B.K.: Thank you, Lagbaja. (*Opening door.*) It is already bright outside.

LAGBAJA (*without haste*): I must hurry. I... I... don' know how this Saturday will turn out for us. Things are ja-gra-ja, Big Miss B.K.

BIG MISS B.K.: How?

LAGBAJA: Times are hard, Big Miss B.K., Jokutor is still out of work.

BIG MISS B.K.: And things are not getting any better here in Obasai. In fact we are heading for worse times and starvation than I have known since I was a child.

LAGBAJA: It is awful. Yesterday, I was expecting some money from Tokumboh.

BIG MISS B.K.: Tokumboh is in a bad state at the moment.

LAGBAJA: You can say that again. I sent Titty-Shine-Shine there three times. I even went there myself.

BIG MISS B.K.: Nothing doing. I know.

LAGBAJA: Her condition is worse than mine. What with her mother who's just died and her husband in hospital dying of cancer. I couldn't press her much.

BIG MISS B.K.: Our elders used to say 'Nar eye for look eye an' feel sorry for each other'.

LAGBAJA: It's true oh, Big Miss B.K. Quite true. How can you help us? It is not for me. If it was me alone. I can manage all right. But with Titty-Shine-Shine and Jokutor... I don't know; but it hurts me to know that my child and husband have to go without food.

BIG MISS B.K. (*consolingly*): The Lord that split our mouths, Lagbaja, will always provide.

LAGBAJA: That's what I always say to myself, and he has never let me down.

BIG MISS B.K.: I don't have much; you know that.

LAGBAJA: Yes, I know that you have your own problems.

BIG MISS B.K.: Still, the little I have here, we can split.

LAGBAJA: I'll return it as soon as I get my money from Tokumboh.

BIG MISS B.K.: Here, I have six pounds plus ten shillings I just gave you to shop for me . . . Take this three pounds.

LAGBAJA: Big Miss B.K.!

BIG MISS B.K.: That will see you through for the weekend, won't it?

LAGBAJA: Thank you. Thank you, Big Miss B.K., thank you so.

BIG MISS B.K.: Never mind, Lagbaja. It's not me you should thank. We are here to help each other. If I have and know that you are in need and I fail to come to your help, I will only be deceiving myself like one of the many who talk about brotherhood, neighbourliness, comradeship and solidarity, et cetera, et cetera. (*Fading.*) I believe in you, Lagbaja, like I trust everybody that I come across. I know that you will come to my aid and rescue, and my children's, if you have the means and power.

LAGBAJA: Gladly too, Big Miss B.K.

BIG MISS B.K.: Go now before the market gets crowded.

SCENE TWO

The village market down the wharf. Typical of any African market where fishermen, fishmongers, hawkers, buyers, thieves, honest, ugly, poor and rich meet. Majekudume is playing cards.

MAJEKUDUME: Take this you win. Take this you loss. Take this win. Take this loss. Look at the cards. See them. This is the win one. Hold it, feel it – good. This win, this loss, this loss, this loss, this win. Try you luck. Good Saturday bargain. One pound for two pounds double your money and buy plenty-plenty for Saturday an' Sunday. Watch the cards fall. Watch. This win, this loss, this loss, this win. Any bet? (*Isaac rushes into the crowd.*)

ISAAC: I bet four pounds for how much?

MAJEKUDUME (*laughs cajolingly*): Ah, good first customer for today.

ISAAC: How much I get if I play four pounds?

MAJEKUDUME: Eight quid, eight quid. Good money... No funny...

VOICE (*from the crowd*): Deal the cards. Stop fooling... business...

MAJEKUDUME (*smoothly*): Easy, man, easy.

ISAAC: O.K. O.K. Lay them cards straight busta. I wah an ol' sea lion. I know quick-triga guys like you.

MAJEKUDUME: Take this you win. Take this you loss. Take this win, take this loss, this loss. This win, dis loss, dis loss, dis loss, dis one. This be the win one. Dis loss, loss, win, loss, win, loss, loss, win, win, win, loss. (*Throws cards one after the other on the ground.*)

ISAAC: Hi! Hi! Man you deal too fast for me eyes to follow you fingers. Too fast... but... as I s ... a ... y... (*Thinking*) Eh... (*To an onlooker.*) Say Mam, Missis. Do pick. Pick up that card lying right in the middle. Go on. Pick it up. Yes Missus, pick it up. Don't panic oh. It is my own sweat and honest labour money. Go on. Pick the middle card.

If I loss. I loss… (*Crowd shows excitement.*) You see, Mama. I have won eight quid. Now, I will give you one quid. You are a lucky Saturday woman.

CROWD: You see everything is luck. God talk for you, mammy. Some people are born with luck. I am going to try my luck this time. You better watch it, ohoooo.

ISAAC: I tell you. I say, I know guys like you. From Lobito to Kotonu, Freetown to Monrovia. Accra to Port Harcourt. All the way I know them. Here Mamma (*ruffle of paper*) take this one pound. Go buy foofoo and bitter-leaf for cook for you Sunday morning col' foofoo chop.

1 ST WOMAN (*anxiously and gratefully*): Thank you, my son. Thank you. Thank you, my son. From where this has come may God double it twice over for you.

MAJEKUDUME: Try you luck. Try you luck. Come on, come on. Take this you win. Take this you loss. This is the win one, this the loss one, this win, this loss, this loss, this win, this win, this loss, this win.

2 ND WOMAN (*shouts*): I play two pounds.

MAJEKUDUME: That's the trick. You get four pounds. This is the win one. This loss, this loss, this win. Look here Mama: this win, this loss, this loss, win, loss, loss, win, loss, loss, win, loss, loss. (*Throws cards. Sound of disappointment from crowd.*) Ahaaaaa! Mama you loss ohhooooo. See, this is the win one. Come on try again ohooooo. This loss, this win, this loss, this win.

A LAYABOUT: Three pounds!

MAJEKUDUME: You get six pounds. Good bet. Now look – look good – this is the win one, this is the loss one, win, loss, loss, win, win, loss.

ISAAC (*shouts*): Hey Majeks, Gbada commin' P.C. Gbep on line. (*Everybody tries to escape. Isaac grabs cards and money and flees. Majekudume makes a last minute desperate escape after him.*)

MAJEKUDUME (*runs and turning to look behind*): Where is he? Where is he?

LAYABOUT (*chasing after them. Shouting*): Catch him! Hold
them. Don't let them escape, they have my three pounds.
Thief, thief. Hey! Hey! Help... thief... help.

CROWD: Where? Where is the thief? (*A crash follows.
Produce and stalls overturn. A typical African market women
reaction.*) Wooooooooooooooooooooooo Wooooooooooooo ...

MALE VOICE (*from crowd*): Do you think I left my house
only to come here and spend my time catching thieves?
Do you think I am crazy like you? Hit-or-miss gambler.

LAYABOUT: Do good people. Help me, help me.

CROWD: Suppose those thieves turn and stab you? Say that
again. I come to sell; not to run after stray thieves. In the
first place, who sent him to come gambling eh? He wants
to earn what he hasn't worked for. He deserves it. Go
mourn your loss old man. This will teach you some sense.
Big man, big fool.

P.C. GBEP (*heavy strides*): All right, all right. Everyday you
get away with something or the other, Majekudume.
Today you've got one on me. Next time you make sure
we don't cross each other. (*Walks towards the crowd.*) A
good hunter does not bring a near-miss-shot game to the
hungry waiting villagers. (*Laughs sardonically.*) I'll get you
into the net, Majekudume, and your mother will not be
able to save a hair of your head. I'll lay my hands on you
and by golly I'll tame you, like you've never been trained
before.

FEMALE VOICE (*from crowd*): P.C. Gbep, goodmornin'
sah.

P.C. GBEP (*coldly*): Thank God it is good for you, maam.

FEMALE VOICE: Yes sah. We are looking forward for whatever blessing Master Jesus will shower on us today.

P.C. GBEP (*under his breath. Going.*): Cackling old monger.
To hell with you all.

SCENE THREE

A street in Obasai. Late morning. Villagers are all going about their business. Children, dogs, sheep all take their time noticing each other.

JOKUTOR (*calling*): Majekudume. Majekudume. (*Running towards them.*) Siiiiiaeeeeeeeeee. Siiiiieeeee. Majeks. Isaac.

MAJEKUDUME (*from a distance*): Hi, Mr Jokutor. What's boiling over?

JOKUTOR (*breathless; approaching*): Wait for me. I've got good news for you.

ISAAC (*to Majeks*): Birds of the same feather flock together. Like his wife, he comes with busybody fas-mot gossips. He always has tidings of great joy. Always when they want either to talk about other people's private affairs or cadge something or want to borrow money, that's how they start. (*Running steps approach.*)

MAJEKUDUME (*cynically calculated*): Forget the damn . . .

JOKUTOR: Majeks. Majeks.

MAJEKUDUME: Easy, bra Jokutor. Easy.

JOKUTOR (*panting breathlessly*): Majeks, I am callin' you, and you just don't wait to listen. This is good fortune for us. We've got a good deal. Good proposition for us.

ISAAC: Who is the good Samaritan, hey bra Jokutor?

MAJEKUDUME: Easy Isaac, easy.

JOKUTOR (*a long pause as they walk along*): Let's go and have a drink somewhere quiet and I'll tell you all about this God-sent fortune. You know, Majeks, a patient dog always get the fattest bone in the end.

ISAAC: Yes. True. But on what does the starving patient dog feed until this fattest of fat bones drops off the greedy plate, bra Jokutor?

MAJEKUDUME: Forget the damn.

JOKUTOR: You think it is a big joke, Majeks? You wait

until you hear all about it. You surely will be the first to game. I know. I can feel it.

MAJEKUDUME: If it is worth my while, yes! I like fat strong bones. My teeth are all strong and ready for the challenge. Now, how about the drink, eh?

JOKUTOR: Yeh. The drinks. Let's go to your sister's bar, Isaac!

ISAAC (*furious*): Go to my sister's bar? Are you out of your mind? You see, bra Jokutor, you and that wife of yours, Lagbaja, you two are the maker and bringer of most troubles in the goddamn hovel of a place called Obasai.

JOKUTOR (*angry*): Mind your words, Isaac. What have I said that you should blaze on me like a noonday fire being blown all over the place by wild winds destroying as it spreads? What have I said that you flame with fury on me and my wife? What?

MAJEKUDUME: Easy, gentlemen. Easy.

ISAAC: You damn well know that I have left home. You and your wife have been going around with the news that I have turned into a wayward street lag. Henchman of Majekudume, the uncontrollable gangster, trickster, gambler and the devil and you know the bloody rest of it all.

JOKUTOR: Isaac, if you think you can talk to me like you talk to your contemporaries . . . (*slaps Isaac*) you are wrong. (*Gives him another slap.*)

ISAAC: You slap me, you slap me. I'll show you that you have no right. (*They grapple.*)

JOKUTOR: How dare you! Upstart. Braggart. Unbrought up . . .

ISAAC: Let go my balls or I'll strangle you. Hi! Hi! Let go.

MAJEKUDUME (*laughing. He separates them*): O.K. cool it. Cool it!

ISAAC (*wild with rage*): Excuse me, Majekudume. I want to put some village sense and puritan respect in . . . come on Jokutor. I challenge you – come.

JOKUTOR: Wait a minute, Majeks. I'll teach him.

MAJEKUDUME: Forget the damn, bra Jokutor.

ISAAC: Come touch me again. I'll beat you with this stick like a snake. Come, come and I'll wager you like a top.

JOKUTOR: You see, Majeks. It is all your fault that he is talking big like that.

ISAAC: You damn corrupt hypocrite gossip. You and your stupid wife make this place a hell for decent people to live and be happy. One dare not move nor speak nor laugh. Everything about everything and everybody in Obasai you know and carry around as if you are so honest, straight, proper and decent.

MAJEKUDUME: Shut your trap and listen. If you two want to have a go at each other, let's go down the wharf. There will be no one there to interfere or go between. I'll be too glad to adjudicate and bring the news to Obasai. How about that?

JOKUTOR: I wouldn't lower my prestige with a scavenger. He is of low pedigree.

ISAAC: Mr High Pedigree, we can see how far you have got in life. It's no surprise that as soon as people see you or your wife approaching, if they are messing up themselves, they sooner sit and hide their mess rather than to ask the likes of you for help of any kind.

JOKUTOR: When I get my hands on you, Isaac, your grandmother will have difficulties to identify you in the hospital. (*From a distance down the road Lagbaja in her usual loudness calls out to Jokutor.*)

LAGBAJA (*calling*): Jokutor! Jokutor! Are you deaf, Jokutor? Joku come here. Jokutor ayaaa!

JOKUTOR: Why the hell are you hollering my name as if I am deaf?

MAJEKUDUME: You run along and meet your wife, bra Jokutor. We'll go to Daddy Jebu's palm-wine cellar and relax.

JOKUTOR (*surprised*): What? But, but your mother will be mad to know that you've started going there.

LAGBAJA: Jokutor, I am waiting. Jokutor . . .

MAJEKUDUME: We'll be waiting for you to get the good tidings and what's more the drink.

ISAAC: And I'll be waiting to see you come finish me up.

MAJEKUDUME: Forget the damn.

ISAAC: Easy, Dad. He's a real punk. Look how he's running to meet the bitch. She wears his trousers and he wears her frock. (*Isaac and Majekudume exit.*)

LAGBAJA (*scoldingly*): Jokutor, I am surprised at you. Everyday you get nearer to something degrading and upsetting for me. What are you doing with those two enh? Didn't I tell you to wait for me at home? What the devil are you doing with those two thieves? What do you want with them? What can they offer you? Jail-house! Can't you choose your company among your equals? Chai! You have ears but they are waxstuck. I sweat day in and day out to keep our home going. Feed you, and clothe you and Titty-Shine-Shine. I struggle for Obasai people not to see and know the worst side of our lives – our disgrace, shame and downfall. But no sooner am not around you wilfully put yourself in the worst company just to spoil the good name I am trying to build.

JOKUTOR: Stop your ridiculous moaning and go home.

LAGBAJA: Moaning? Am I, ehn! I wish P.C. Gbep had caught the three of you, then perhaps you would have felt the sweetness of my moaning.

JOKUTOR: Every time you go out, there is always something to grumble and complain about. What is all this about, now?

LAGBAJA; No, don't ask me. I grumble and complain. Go and ask your good companions. They will tell you what they have been up to this morning down the market. Go on. Go ask them to split with you the three pounds they stole and the rest of the money they won. Go Mr Big Man Big Fool.

JOKUTOR (*desperately*): Lagbaja, you always make a mountain out of nothing.

LAGBAJA: I don't blame you. You can talk to me as you like. You enjoy your lazy life. You know that whether you work or not, there'll always be food for you to stuff your guts. I don't blame you at all. I blame myself. Fool that I am.

JOKUTOR (*bursts out with anger*): I have done the same for you. And more. You know that. And it was then for me a pleasure. So now woman, don't you go treating me like a child. Don't talk to me as if you were the one who married me. Hear? Understand? (*Dramatically.*) I married you. I am master of my house. Until I die, or something else happens to alter and separate our lives, as such that we have to decide otherwise; I still remain the ruling-head of the house. (*Angrily.*) Now to hell with you and your P.C. Gbep et cetera, et cetera. I am going to do exactly as I like. And from now on. (*Going.*)

LAGBAJA (*rather exasperated*): Jokutor. You, you . . .

JOKUTOR: I am old enough to see and know what is good from what is bad. (*Exit.*)

LAGBAJA (*contemplatively walking away. Talks to herself*): Well! Obasai devil seem bent on disrupting as many lives in Obasai this year. What on earth is happening? What is happening to us in Obasai! Some people are running away from the country, others are dying, running mad, going from bad to worst. What is wrong with us? Everything is crooked and difficult. We are all looking at each other with hate and reacting with passionate viciousness. Thank God I am all right.

SCENE FOUR

It is mid-afternoon at Big Miss B.K.'s house. Sound of laughter. Glasses clinking. A merry atmosphere, but not too jolly or boisterous. General laughter. Rather moderate in tone and quality.

REV. J.J.T. (*very nasal and pedantic*): Yes! Welcome back home, Logan. We have been expecting you since Thursday.

LOGAN (*eager and enthusiastic, very confident*): The roads are awfully bad, Revren' J.J.T., and especially now that it has started to rain.

BIG MISS B.K.: And the rains have been very heavy this past two weeks.

REV. J.J.T.: We are glad God's breeze took you away and brought you back safe to us, Logan. Blessed be the name of the Lord.

ALL: Amen. Praise be to his name.

REV. J.J.T.: East, West, North or South; home is best.

BIG MISS B.K.: Say that again, Rev. J.J.T., say it again.

REV. J.J.T. (*sighs heavily. Gulps down his drink*): Ha, yes; the Lord maketh poor and rich; he bringeth low, and lifteth up. Remember how hard things were for you in the last two years, Logan? (*They re-fill J.J.T.'s glass with drink.*)

LOGAN (*with a sigh*): Yes, Revren'.

REV. J.J.T.: Do you remember my words to you then? 'He that is down needs fear no fall. He that is low no pride.' Logan, we are glad that you are back with us. We know what you have seen and learnt in this very short time that you have been away. All that you have acquired, you will share with us. You are a great and good example to us here in Obasai. You are . . .

(*A loud and continuous knocking on the door.*)

BIG MISS B.K.: Come in. Come in.

AJAYI (*enters. She is moody and temperamental*): Afternoon Revren', Mr Logan, Big Miss B.K. If you are busy you will have to excuse me because I have just about had enough.

REV. J.J.T. (*rather concerned*): What is it, Ajayi?

LOGAN: Why don't you sit down?

AJAYI (*abruptly*): No sah, thank you. You see Revren' J.J.T., my brother Isaac ran away from home some two weeks now. My grandmother and I have tried to get him to come home but he has flatly refused because Majekudume has been ill-advising him. Telling him that it is better to be poor and free than to have everything and be kept like a dog in a kennel.

LOGAN: What?

BIG MISS B.K.: Lord have mercy. This Majekudume will kill me.

AJAYI: Lagbaja came to our house this morning and told grandma that Isaac has ganged up with Majekudume gambling down wharf market. This has upset grandma and now I am the one who is spared no peace nor rest.

LAGBAJA (*entering*): What I told you Ajayi is the God's truth. In fact this morning when I went to the market Big Miss B.K., – are you hearing me sah, Revren'? I met Majekudume and Isaac surrounded by a crowd of people. They were busy playing 'Winnie and Lossie' card gambling. Mr Logan you know the kind of game sah.

LOGAN: Go on Lagbaja.

REV. J.J.T.: Carry on.

LAGBAJA: Isaac and Majekudume are so versed in the game that they easily bribe ignorant poor people to play. For instance, Isaac pretended as if he was new to the whole business. He played four pounds and Majekudume gave him eight pounds in return. In order to coax other people to lose their money, Isaac gave an old woman one pound. Of yes. I saw it all. Majekudume is the boss and Isaac his peggy-boy. This morning I saw them win lots of money. Then P.C. Gbep came and they fled. This is what I think was unbearable. They took three pounds from a poor man who was about to play and run away with it. Is that not bad name Revren'? Is that not a disgrace to their families? To us all here in Obasai? I mean, we all love them like our own children. Whatever happens, we don't want to see them get into any trouble. Do we? I mean, Big Miss B.K., just as soon as I returned from market did I not say that I overheard them saying that they are going to that medicine man, Daddy Jebu's, palm-wine drinking cellar?

AJAYI (*rather sardonically*): What's wrong with Daddy Jebu's palm-wine drinking cellar, Lagbaja?

LAGBAJA: You tell me. Is that a decent place for good free-born Obasai educated children?

REV. J.J.T.: Certainly not.

AJAYI: Revren' J.J.T., you surprise me. You mean to say, sah, that after all these years it has not yet come to your notice that some of your staunch members who go to church every Sunday, receive Holy Communion and pay their collections and sing hallellujah and hosannah.

REV. J.J.T.: They praise their maker, Ajayi.

AJAYI (*sarcastically*): After they have prayed to their maker with all their hypocritical reverence they can muster, they also go to Daddy Jebu to hold the 'Thunder hammer' in readiness to strike their neighbour and shout 'crucify'. Ask Lagbaja. She knows everything about everything and everybody. And more so about herself.

REV. J.J.T.: Ajayi what is all this about.

AJAYI (*muttering*): That's what I came to find out. Goodbye. (*She slams the door behind her.*)

LAGBAJA: Don't break the door, Ajayi. I'd better get back to the kitchen and see that the sauce doesn't get burnt.

BIG MISS B.K.: O.K., Lagbaja.

LAGBAJA: I only came in to confirm that what she was going to say was exactly as I told her. People get easily carried away these days and as such they easily add pepper and salt to make other people's stories seem more spicy than it should normally taste. I wouldn't like to be misunderstood. Would you Revren'?

REV. J.J.T.: No. It creates the wrong impression and leaves bad ideas mixed up in people's minds.

LAGBAJA: Exactly. And that's what I'd hate to happen to me. (*She goes.*)

BIG MISS B.K. (*in tears*): Revren' J.J.T., why does it always have to be my Majekudume? Why, why? He is a bad boy, I know that. I do not condone him. You all know how much I have tried to help him to a better life. Still people are not prepared to let him alone. No one, no mother will exchange their bad child for a good one. Majekudume has been accused by everyone in Obasai. Some call him a thief, a rogue, a scavenger. Others brand him as a rascal, layabout, pimp and all sorts of bad name. Yet he has not stabbed or killed anyone. He has not raped anybody's daughter or coveted their wives. What has he done that the whole of Obasai hate him so much?

LOGAN: Not everybody hates Majekudume, Big Miss B.K. If they did, they could have easily harm him. Strong and brave though he may be. Don't loose your faith in people because of Majekudume. He'll change in time and people will get to know and like his personality. He is a little different and people are not easily tolerant of what is not of their own likeness and image.

REV. J.J.T.: You talk in parables Logan. There is much sense in what you have just said.

BIG MISS B.K.: When will he change? How will he change? Will it be for the worse? Now he has started to go to witch-doctor's palm-wine cellar. Where will he go next? Where?

LOGAN: Don't worry Big Miss B.K., I am back. Leave everything to me. I'll sort them out good and proper. I'll fix Majekudume up. Don't you worry.

REV. J.J.T.: That's what I like to hear Logan. That's why I like you. You are a man of strong willpower and clear determination. My faith in you has never faltered. Never.

SCENE FIVE

Noisy African bar. Some drunk, some half drunk and some voices singing off key with strained notes trying to achieve a harmonious crescendo. Lazy dancing, feet shuffling and beating on the hard floor.

MAJEKUDUME, ISAAC AND JOKUTOR (*singing loudly. For music see p. 38*):

How you yone tan sooooooo?
nar by you way
How you yone tan soooo
nar by you way
How you yone tan soooo
nar by you way
nar by you way
nar by you way

MAJEKUDUME:

How me yone tan so

ALL:

nar by you way

MAJEKUDUME:

How me yone spoil so

ALL:

nar by you way

MAJEKUDUME:

If A' bad too mus'
nor to me smell pass all
una do ya lef me make A' go me way.

ALL (*they La-la to the tune*): La-la-la-la-la-la-la-la-la.

JOKUTOR (*shouting*): Daddy Jebu bring over here, one bottle Dynamite gin. Six Moon-star beer and one packet Habana.

ISAAC: This is no joking matter. He's commin' over here.

MAJEKUDUME: Easy does it, man. Cool it, baby boy.

JOKUTOR (*with excitement*): P.C. Gbep.

P.C. GBEP: That's me all over. Rock and roll. Never tire.

MAJEKUDUME: Easy.

JOKUTOR: Anything wrong around the joint?

P.C. GBEP: Check-in. Check-out. Keep folks happy.

MAJEKUDUME: Easy.

JOKUTOR: P.C. Gbep sit down. We have some exceptional good news. It will interest you. Sit down.

DADDY-JEBU (*approaching*): Ha! I see we have P.C. Constable visit us today. Daddy-Jebu gettin' famous, eh?

Someday Daddy-Jebu will do great things for Obasai. Maybe someday Daddy-Jebu will Jagae-butu, jagae-tinap for P.C. Constable. (*Rolls his tongue.*)

P.C. GBEP: Yes, Daddy-Jebu. Someday when I do have an overweighing and unsolved problem I will come to you. And of course with necessary consultation fees. For now, let it just be check-in, check-out.

DADDY-JEBU: You want drink, P.C. Constable?

P.C. GBEP: Eh, well. Just water.

JOKUTOR (*teasing*): You know the kind of water, eh, Daddy-Jebu?

DADDY-JEBU (*they both laugh*): I know Water-water, well and proper from palm stick-belly. Good for P.C. Constable. (*In the meantime Isaac has escaped, gone to sit by the piano. He fidgets with the keys and starts playing a tune. He shouts to the others to be attentive.*)

ISAAC: Hey! Hey! You all listen to my new and latest composition. (*Shouts.*) Silence! Listen to my genius at work. (*He plays introductory chords. He begins to sing. After a while the others join in the singing. For music see p. 38.*)

ISAAC (*singing*):

If you don't want progress

ALL:

Go nar Obasai

ISAAC:

If you want to take bride

ALL:

Walk down Obasai

ISAAC:

If you have some power

ALL:

Make for Obasai.
Make all man opin yie,
nar Obasai ohoooooooo
Make all man opin yie,
nar Obasai ohoooooo.

ALL:
Can you do some smuggling
Come to Obasai.
Can you tell good fortune
Swing down Obasai.
Do you like Mercedes
Pump for Obasai.
Are you good with women
Lots in Obasai
Make all man opin yie
Nar Obasai ohhhooooo
Make all man opin yie
Nar Obasai ooohhooooooo.
(*Crowd shouts and claps.*)

P.C. GBEP: That Isaac boy has got good and mischievous talents. Womanizing, money grabbin' and pianoing – the lot.

MAJEKUDUME (*drunkenly*): Forget the damn P.C. Gbep.

DADDY-JEBU (*bursting with enthusiasm*): I too, I can sing. Now I will sing for you Daddy-Jebu best song. Yes!

CROWD (*very noisy*): Yes. Yes. Yes. Daddy-Jebu will sing.

DADDY-JEBU (*for music see p. 39*):
Kondo Bai Goyoo
Kondo Bai Goyoo
Gee Ya Mu Taelur
Ven dee Van Da Van Da Van Da
Ven Dee Van Da Jawa Ja 'Aaa
Ha Van 'gay Mangi
Van 'gay Yah Van 'gay
    Mangi
Van 'gay Yah Van 'gay
Me Mamma buy Kunu
Ku Wrengbeh
Ku Wrengbeh Wrengbeh
    Ku Wrengbeh
KeeNee Gbash-Gbash

VaVa Yomboye Va
KeeNee Gbash-Gbash
VaVa Yomboye Va

Kondo Bai Goyoo
Kondo Bai Goyoo
Gee Ya Mu Taelur
VenDee Vanda Jawa Ja 'Aaa
Ha Van 'gay Mangi
Van 'gay Van 'gay Van 'gay Van 'gay
Ha Van 'gay Yaaaaa Van 'gay
    Mangi
Van 'gay Ya-Yah Van 'gayaaaa.
    (*Crowd laughter and clapping continues. Voices in the back-ground continue to hum the tune as they go and come.*)

P.C. GBEP: Well, I must be on my way.

DADDY-JEBU (*approaching*): P.C. Constable goin' now?

P.C. GBEP: Yes, Daddy-Jebu. Duty calls you know.

DADDY-JEBU (*rather over excited*): Don't go now. I bring you this drink. For you and my very good comrades here, Mr Jokutor, Majekudume an' Isic.

P.C. GBEP: Very kind of you Daddy-Jebu. But it is against the rules of the game.

DADDY-JEBU: But the game has not started. Why begin to think about rules? Drink and enjoy.

JOKUTOR: Sit down, P.C. Gbep. You know as well as I do that –

P.C. GBEP: That what?

JOKUTOR: That you can bend the law; as long as you do not break it, you are all right.

P.C. GBEP (*sitting down again*): You are not a very good friend, Jokutor.

MAJEKUDUME: Easy, P.C. Gbep. Easy.

ISAAC: This kind of goodness does not happen every day.

DADDY-JEBU: Now, I will sit next to my good friend Isic. Yes?

ISAAC: Of course, Daddy-Jebu. We are the best of friends.

DADDY-JEBU (*scraping his throat*): Mr Jokutor . . . tch . . . what do we say?

P.C. GBEP: Cheers and good luck.

DADDY-JEBU: No. In my custom, we invite the dead to guide over us. We implore them to help us and keep watch over all that we do and say. We ask their blessing and beg them not to be angry with us when we foolishly go wrong in our naïve ways towards each other. Amina. (*They all drink.*)

JOKUTOR: That is our real African tradition.

P.C. GBEP: My parents used to pour libation. But with all this change and Independence and Western way of life, we too have changed unknowingly.

ISAAC: Pouring libation is waste of good liquor.

MAJEKUDUME: Forget the dead. Forget the damn.

DADDY-JEBU: Well, Mr Jokutor, I, eh, I have good news for you, maybe; perhaps it will be bad news for those people who don't like me.

JOKUTOR (*jumps to his feet*): Ha! Daddy-Jebu, you can't beat me to the game. Let me tell them. I was only waiting for you to be present and for the place to clear a little. Well, I know that this will come as a surprise to you all gentlemen. Yes . . . (*He belches.*) Just over a week ago, I had a solitary shilling in my pocket. To tell you the truth, that was all I had, and could boast of as a married man with a wife and a daughter of seventeen years old. Only this shilling was my savings. As you all know my mother is alive and old. I have sisters and brothers. All of them look up to me and expect something from me. However small. Well, I stroll around. I didn't know where to go. At last the wind turned me to this direction. I came in here to drink. Not to talk to anyone. No. I wanted to be alone. To find out why I was the only one who seems not to be able to find any practical solution for my present state. Jobless, moneyless and unhappiness.

ISAAC: Is it the gospel according to St Jokutor?

MAJEKUDUME: Forget the damn. Get to the good tidings, bra Jokutor.

JOKUTOR: O.K.! O.K.! Well, as I was sitting here enjoying my drink quite absentmindedly, Daddy-Jebu came up to me. The bar was deserted. He put his hand on my shoulder. Well, I was frightened at first not knowing what he was about. I was repulsed and felt like pushing him strong and fast and make my way out quick.

ISAAC: Yes. All those bad things that the people of Obasai have been talking about him came to you like noonday rainbow. Bright and clear . . .

MAJEKUDUME: You thought he was going to witch-doctor you like they say he does to the pregnant women and young babies who die daily in Obasai.

JOKUTOR: Exactly. However, I don't know what stopped me. Instinct maybe. (*Pause.*) He is a human being like us all, if not better. Yes, I looked at the hand on my shoulder. It was strong and firm and warm. I raised my head; and comrades, when my eyes and Daddy-Jebu's met, I saw and felt nothing but pity. In his eyes I could see hate, fear, loneliness and compassion. I went cold.

ISAAC: Your record has finished?

JOKUTOR: You take pleasure in being rude; don't you, Isaac?

P.C. GBEP: You went cold and?

JOKUTOR: And so we sat and talked our hearts out.

MAJEKUDUME: You mean, you drank you guts full. Order some more drinks.

DADDY-JEBU: Yes. Yes. I will supply the drinks. Same for everybody, eh? (*Going.*)

JOKUTOR: To cut long story short. Daddy-Jebu explained that since most of the people in Obasai do not like him, he is determined to show them that he has no dislike for anyone. Nor does he bear grudge against those who malign his name. In fact he intends to open up a big project which he asked me to advise him about. So that's how our friendship started. And since we want to go ahead with the project, I have tried to get my good friend Majekudume on our side.

MAJEKUDUME: And what will I be doing?

JOKUTOR: If you game, man, you will be doing just what is good for you. What you want.

MAJEKUDUME: I don't buy pigs in pen. Tell us more about this gigantic project.

ISAAC: And your wise advice too.

JOKUTOR: Well, Obasai is primarily a fishing village and we are blessed with three wharves, a beautiful bay and the wide open river full of fishes.

MAJEKUDUME: So?

JOKUTOR: I advise him to start a fishing business.

ISAAC: That's practical and honest advice. Good show Mr Jokutor, for once.

DADDY-JEBU: And I have bought a big, big trawler. It is standing on the water, down the bay. You can start fishing today, any day you like.

MAJEKUDUME: That's just the thing I've been dreaming about. Now, Daddy-Jebu, I am on your pay-roll; port or starboard?

ISAAC: Who is the Skipper-Jack?

JOKUTOR (*beaming*): Me. I am an old hand in the trade.

ISAAC: Well, Mr Skipper, I beg to apply for apprenticeship under you able supervision, sir.

P.C. GBEP: This will be a knock-out for some of our fat-mouthed big men who go around bluffing year in year out. A real knock-out!

ISAAC: About time we get some men of active blood in this damn Obasai. People who do things and not just keep talking and promising motically.

P.C. GBEP: Since I joined the police twenty-five years ago, I am still stripeless. And could you believe, if I tell you that my wage is twenty-one pound, thirteen shillings

and ninepence. I have a wife and eight children to look
after.

MAJEKUDUME (*coming awake again*): You must realize that
you are Mr Gbep. You are a representative of the many
little fishes scattered all over the country. All very nicely
swallowed and forgotten. No matter how very hard you
will try P.C. Gbep, you should always remember that
you are not one of the chosen few. You were born unlucky.
You should have been born and named Mr Mason-Cole;
Mr Tobias Streeter; Son of Sir Ade Tokumboh Emanuel
Lewis-Scott. What a pity you chose the wrong womb!
You see me. All people can do with me is to complain.
Nothing more. I am still here. If I had not been born by
Big Miss B.K., I know where I could have been by now.
When you have power take as much advantage of people
and the rotten world as you like. For when the time
comes for them to rebel, there will be nothing left for you
to hang on to. I feel sorry for people like you P.C. Gbep.
You see, you didn't go to the right school. You were not
fortunate to have attended the proper university. Or
should I ask with impertinence, what efforts have you
made to pave your way to get in? How do you intend to
get to the top? Rome was not built in a day you know.
You must pay your way.

P.C. GBEP: How?

ISAAC: Maybe by donating your beautiful sister? Sacrificing
your charming daughter? Or just trademark your niece;
let her glide along to any one of the top dogs . . . them
higher echelons . . .

MAJEKUDUME: If not, deliver your wage to your immediate
boss who would be too pleased to help bring your files
up-to-date. Or to be a little faster in the move, try to be a
much more tolerant fellow and allow your wife, if she is
chick and prim, to be exquisitely indulgent.

ISAAC: After all she has been your wife. Let another man
satisfy his curiosity and whet his appetite.

B

P.C. GBEP (*furious and upset*): Lord have mercy. I will chop off that man's head with a matchet. Any damn man – King, Commander or President.

ISAAC: There is no hope for you to rise. No hope for the likes of you.

P.C. GBEP: I don't care. If I don't rise, I won't fall either.

JOKUTOR: P.C. Gbep. He who says, I don't care, cares very much indeed. Don't care was made to care. You should know that by now.

P.C. GBEP: I cannot continue with this kind of conversation. It upsets me. I think I'd better be on my way.

MAJEKUDUME: Yes. You had better be, P.C. Gbep. And the first person you happen to meet, tell him or her to tell Lagbaja that we, I mean all of us here, including our master, Daddy-Jebu, tell them, that we have decided to secede from the rest of Obasai. Now we are going to try our own strength against the big raging sea, against which we cannot defend ourselves. We have decided not to go on believing their motical promises. When they give us with one hand they come back to collect with two hands. We, as from today refuse to accept any more dictates of decadence with which Obasai reeks. Daddy-Jebu has given us the confidence we lack. He has come out as a man of action. One who believes in hard work whether it be killing by medicine or thieving or whatever the good old something offers to hold on to. And we are prepared to hold fast, to fight, sustain and keep it.

ISAAC: Tell them that we have got our strength and courage from the worst of the despised rejects. Now we are prepared to disown our good and blessed homes and parents. Daddy-Jebu, the reject of their church, state, society and morals, is now our saviour. We, as young rejects from the good old society, have now realized how best to judge the respectable human kind. In short we have now teamed up with the reject. The heathen they accuse of bowing down to wood and stone.

MAJEKUDUME: We promise we will plague them no more with our idleness, rudeness, badness and sinness. We will not give you cause to go chasing us. Go tell them in your own words, P. C. Gbep. Tell it all like a good old and well-trained policeman who believes in the truth and justice of every free mortal being.

DADDY-JEBU: It is enough. I think that the police constable understands our feelings and knows that we are genuine in our undertaking and comradeship.

P.C. GBEP: They are my feelings too. Only I am too old, too tired to start all over again. But in spirit, I am with you all the way – all the way.

DADDY-JEBU: In that case, I want to tell you, my friends and co-partners. I am going to get married. That is my own news. I am going to be married today. Here and before your eyes. I should have done it long ago, but I have no friends to come and help me drink and eat and celebrate. What is more we both wanted our friends' approval. We wanted witnesses, even though it is going to be as primitive and as old as when my great, great, great-grandfather paid his dowry for my great, great, great-grandmother. You my friends, comrades and co-partners, I hope you will not desert me. I hope that our bond of friendship will urge and force us together, to help each other in times of difficulties, differences and troubles.

JOKUTOR: Who is the lucky bride?

DADDY-JEBU: I don't know if I should tell you here and now. You see, marriage sometimes starts hatred and breaks strong friendship.

ISAAC: Sometimes it strengthens the bond of friendship.

DADDY-JEBU (*affectionately*): Will you give me your right hand always, Isic?

ISAAC: Yes. Why not? (*Gives his hand.*)

DADDY-JEBU: Most people give willingly but reservedly.

ISAAC: You shouldn't let them worry you.

JOKUTOR (*laughing*): You are young and boastful Isaac. You know very little about life.

ISAAC: What do you mean?

DADDY-JEBU (*shyly*): I am going to marry your sister. (*They all laugh except Isaac.*)

ISAAC (*puzzled*): Oh yes? (*He smiles and braves it out.*) I see. Well let's celebrate. It's not a funeral. If she agrees, I accept.

P.C. GBEP: Excuse me one and all. I must push off.

JOKUTOR: Don't go yet, P.C. Gbep. We will all be going to welcome Mr Logan when we leave here.

ISAAC: Besides you have to represent the rest of Obasai in my sister's marriage feast with Daddy-Jebu. Someone they can believe must be here to tell them that it was all smooth and sweet and graceful, like any other society-accepted matrimony.

MAJEKUDUME: Easy. We are in no hurry; we don't want to disturb the peacefulness of Revren' J.J.T. and Mr Logan. When we see them we will pay our respects as we have never done before. Talk to them nicely-nicely.

ISAAC: Give our news in brief and take our pleasant leave.

MAJEKUDUME: For better or worse. In success or failure.

DADDY-JEBU: Let us all make merry. My bride will soon arrive. Let us be happy for that is what most people don't know how to be.

SCENE SIX

Big Miss B.K.'s house, as in scene four.

REV. J.J.T. (*eagerly. Talking non-stop*): Now, now Logan, as you have returned with so many good and progressive ideas, I suggest, that is between you and me, I suggest that we spare two hours every evening together. We must plan a better social, moral and practical Obasai for the good and benefit of us all. It will, in the end, be worth every ounce of our time, effort and energy.

LOGAN: Fact.

REV. J.J.T.: Now, Logan, maybe you don't know this, but there are some members in the church who have been in arrears with their Class-dues, Pew-rent, Obasai special Sunday fund, Village Cess fund, Church and Organ fund, Church Renovation fund, Harvest working committee contributions, Dorcas and Mothers Union fund, Special Offertory and Cemetery Cleaning fund.

LOGAN: They must pay up, if we are to face our problems squarely and tackle them soberly.

REV. J.J.T.: Logan, we must help to recover and re-organize the lost and stray among us. We must help them to know what they should make of their lives. Teach them to develop their minds and intellect through the teachings of our Lord Jesus Christ. They must realize that life does not just mean drink, get drunk and run around each other like untrained dogs free to ravel, mess about and fight.

(Drunk shouting and singing approaching from a distance. For music see p. 40.)

MAJEKUDUME, ISAAC AND JOKUTOR *(singing.)*

Mr Logan don kam ohhhoooo
Don kam don kam oooohhhhoooo
Mr Logan kabor ohoo
Kabor, kabor oohhooo
Pa-pa Logan welcome home
welcome, welcome home.

(Singing continues in the background.)

LOGAN: Which of course eventually leads them to the police cell and sometimes to the jail house.

VOICES *(getting nearer)*:

Papa Logan God bring you
Good God bring you home
Papa Logan you look fresh
look whey you rogu.
papa Logan how the trek
welcome, kabor oohhooo

REV. J.J.T. You have got visitors Logan.

LOGAN: Quite a good turn out it seems. (*They enter the house singing – Majekudume, Isaac, Jokutor and P. C. Gbep. Daddy-Jebu stays out with Ajayi.*)

VOICES: Welcome home, Mr Logan.

LOGAN: Come in. Come in everybody.

VOICES: How did you enjoy the trip? What have you brought for us Mr Logan? My. Oh my! You have grown fat. Did they treat you well?

LOGAN (*replies appropriately to every question*): They are a fine people. Very kind and hospitable.

MAJEKUDUME (*comes forward*): And where is my darling mother, Big Miss B.K. Mother! (*Shouts.*) Big Miss B.K.!

BIG MISS B.K. (*enters*): Majekudume! What kind of rudeness is this? Look at you. You are drunk.

MAJEKUDUME: Never mind me, Mother dear. Where is my baby brother, Wokhog? (*Shouts.*) Wokhog! Where are you, mamma's pet?

JOKUTOR (*belches long and loud*): My, that was a good wind let out. Sorry, good people, but you cannot suppress nature.

LAGBAJA: Jokutor, you are disgusting. You are pssst.

MAJEKUDUME: Mother dear, I can see you are happy. Mr Logan is back.

JOKUTOR: Lagbaja what are you doing here?

BIG MISS B.K.: Jokutor, Lagbaja has been helping me. I don't know how I could have managed without her.

JOKUTOR (*rudely*): Good. It's good to know that she can make herself useful sometimes. (*They all laugh.*)

LAGBAJA: I don't blame you. I blame those who have been stuffing your gizzard with rum. (*She gives out a long hiss.*)

MAJEKUDUME: Ladies and gentlemen. (*Mockingly.*) Thus saith the Lord God of Hossana; that when two or three are gathered he always grant their request.

REV. J.J.T.: I see you have not forgotten your Bible, Majekudume.

MAJEKUDUME: It's more than that, Revren' J.J.T., I have also just discovered that I have not forgotten what I want out of life.

JOKUTOR: Me also.

ISAAC: And me too.

REV. J.J.T.: Tell us more, gentlemen.

MAJEKUDUME: Fishermen.

JOKUTOR: Fishermen.

ISAAC: Fishermen.

BIG MISS B.K.: Lord have mercy what kind of a child have I brought into this world. (*Desperate*) Fisherman!

LAGBAJA: You were born the day when death struck Shame, Jokutor. You are finished. We are finished.

JOKUTOR: Go in peace, Lagbaja. Where is Daddy Jebu?

ISAAC: He is outside with Ajayi.

MAJEKUDUME (*calls out*): Daddy-Jebu, come in.

REV. J.J.T. (*protesting*): Logan, you will have to excuse me if they are going to invite that ungodly wretch in here.

BIG MISS B.K.: The demon knows his place Revren' J.J.T. He wouldn't dare come in here.

REV. J.J.T.: God forbid I should be under the same roof with a child of Satan.

MAJEKUDUME: Easy, Revren' J.J.T. Easy. This is my mother's house. My father built it. He died. So will my mother. Die. You too, Revren', will die and so will the child of Satan. And so will I.

JOKUTOR: So will all of us.

MAJEKUDUME (*sarcastically*): I like your tolerence Revren' J.J.T. I am happy you can love your neighbour as you love yourself. It is good mother, that you prefer to satisfy a man of God and neglect me, your son. I hope you will all go to heaven. Don't worry, I won't hold on to your skirt, or even your cassock Revren', for you to save me from the everlasting dungeon where fire and brimstone will roast and burn my insides out.

ISAAC: I am going out to join Daddy-Jebu. There seems to

be no more welcome in the democratic way, left in this house.

MAJEKUDUME: Goodbye, Mother. I prefer to join in with the ungodly wretch.

JOKUTOR: Better see eye to eye with the child of Satan than back and bite with the children of paradise.

LAGBAJA: What will the neighbours say?

JOKUTOR: Exactly what you want them to say.

MAJEKUDUME: Let them say what they like.

ISAAC: Fas-Mot Lagbaja you are good as an information officer. Pass on the news. We need all the publicity we can get. Tell the whole of Obasai that my sister, Ajayi, got married to the notorious witch-doctor, Daddy-Jebu, today.

MAJEKUDUME: Easy.

JOKUTOR: We are just coming from the reception at Daddy-Jebu's palm-wine cellar, where he and Ajayi just got married.

P.C. GBEP: I saw it all happen. Native and grand and traditional.

LAGBAJA: Lord have mercy. (*She faints.*)

ISAAC (*laughs*): Lagbaja faints with shock.

MAJEKUDUME: Forget the damn. They are all hypocrites. (*He goes out.*)

REV. J.J.T.: You mean that good, good educated girl got married to that *thing* most vile?

LOGAN: May the good Lord deliver us from evil temptations.

ISAAC: You don't know, sirs, ma'ams, how much we appreciate that you all have been so little shocked and unshaken.

MAJEKUDUME (*calls from outside*): Isaac, Mr Jokutor, let's go. Mother dear, I am glad you can laugh and be happy with Mr Logan, Rev. J.J.T. and Wokhog. They are your type. I have chosen mine. Goodbye. I must go and try to cast my net. Time is against me; but the tide seems to be in our favour. Come on you lot.

JOKUTOR: Lagbaja, you have decided. So have I. Now, it is everyone for himself and God for us all. However, if we are to succeed, which I am sure we will, things for us might take a different turn. Bye, and do take good care of Titty-Shine-Shine.

BIG MISS B.K. (*calls out*): Majekudume, don't go, don't go – Majekudume! (*Calling in strained voice nearing tears.*) Come back, Majeks. Come back.

LOGAN: Let him go, Big Miss B.K. Let him go.

BIG MISS B.K. (*in tears*): Must I sacrifice my son to become a fisherman? Must I? I laboured to give him a good education. All his friends, his contemporaries are responsible office holders. Some have gone to England and others to America. Why should he make a scapegoat of himself?

LAGBAJA: What will people say?

BIG MISS B.K.: He is a well educated child from a good and respectable family. Why should he end up being a fisherman? Why?

LOGAN (*consolingly*): Peter, the great follower of Christ, started as a fisherman. He caught fishes, then converted people and ended up as the first Saint.

REV. J.J.T.: Have courage, Big Miss B.K. Be of good cheer.

BIG MISS B.K. (*desperately*): I can't let him go Revren' J.J.T. I love my son. However bad and spoilt he may be, I can't live to see him waste his life like this.

LOGAN: He has decided. Don't stand in his way.

LAGBAJA (*rather frustrated*): What shall I say? Where do I start from here? To whom do I turn to now, in times of necessity?

REV. J.J.T.: The Lord will provide, Lagbaja. The Lord will provide.

BIG MISS B.K.: Revren' J.J.T., please come help me persuade Majekudume not to go. Please!

REV. J.J.T. (*choked*): I . . . I just can't do it this time Big Miss B.K. You know it is impossible. Please understand and forgive me.

BIG MISS B.K. (*her tears become bitter and her crying hysterical*):
Please, please, Revren' J.J.T. Mr. Logan, please . . .

REV. J.J.T.: You know I have always done everything you
ask me to help you with Big Miss B.K. I would do anything for you. But this time . . . I really am sorry.

BIG MISS B.K.: Mr Logan, Lagbaja. (*Shouts.*) Why don't you
answer? Answer. Answer. (*She rushes out.*)

I alone know the pinches of my shoes. I alone know the pain.

WOKHOG: Mother, Mother let me come with you.

SCENE SEVEN

*The bay. Fade in on heavy seaside wind. Strong waves beating on
the seashore.*

JOKUTOR (*shouting*): Hi!

MAJEKUDUME: Hee-up.

JOKUTOR: All hands on deck.

ISAAC: Ya-ha-huuuuuuu.

ALL: Hee-up

MAJEKUDUME: Hee-up. Pull!

ALL: Hee-up. Pull. Push! (*As they work, they begin to sing.
For music see p. 40.*)

DADDY-JEBU:
Du-Du kam-take kam-take
Du-Du kam take the thing you want

ALL:
Jokutor pull way, pull way
Majeku raise the anchor up.

JOKUTOR:
Hee-upp. Hee-up.

DADDY-JEBU:
Du-Du da-go, da-go
Du-Du da-go, da-go, da-go
Jokutor pull way, pull way
Jokutor steer out to sea
Majeku start now . . . start now

Majeku start to throw the net.

BIG MISS B.K. (*calls. Standing on the rocks*): Majeku, Majeku. My son Majekudume, come back. Come back, I beg you.

WOKHOG (*reassuringly*): We are too late Mother. But he will come back to us. He will. (*He starts to cry.*)

BIG MISS B.K. (*to herself*): Yes, he will come back, someday! Maybe I will live to see him return. Maybe?

(*The movement of the waves grows stronger and the lashing is heavier and more frequent. The crying dies out. We hear faintly the singing from a distance amidst the waves.*)

VOICES (*singing*):
Jokutor pull way, pull way
Majeku go on cast your net
Jokutor pull way, pull way
Jokutor pull us out to sea
Majeku go on, go,
Majeku, this is our chance
(*Obasai lament swells in softly in the distance.*)

VOICES: Hu-hu-huuuuu.

VOICE: Hu-uuuuuuu.

VOICES: Don't pine too much-huuuuuu.

VOICE: Hu-uuuuu.

VOICES: Leave your problems to God-Huuuuu.

VOICE: Huuuuu.

VOICES: He will help you out-huuuuuu.

VOICE: Hu-uuuuuuuuu.

VOICES: Well God Bless-Huuuuu.

VOICE: Huuuu.

Ko- ndo Bai Goyoo
Ko- ndo Bai Goyoo

Gee ya mu Tac- lur

Ven- Dee Van- Da Van- .Da Van- Da

Ven- Dee Van- Da Jawa ja Aaa

Ha Van'-gay Ma- ngi

Ha Van'- gay aaa

Ha Van'gay Ma- ngi

✱2nd. ending

Ha Van'- gay   Ha Van'-gay

Me Ma- mma buy ku- nu
Kee Nee   Gbash Gbash

Then go to beginning
and end on ✱

Ku – Wre-ngbeh Ku – Wre- ngbeh Ku – Wre-ngbeh
Va   Va —   Yomboye   Va —

each verse is
a couplet

Mis - ter Lo- gan don kam oohhooo

repeat until verses
are finished

Don kam don kam ooohhhoo

1st. verse

Du- du Kam take Kam take

Du- du Kam take the thing you want

Jo ku for pull way pull way

Ma- je ku raise the an- chor up

Alla Gbah

CHARACTERS

STUDENT, *Joko Campbell's 'Id'*
JOKO CAMPBELL, *27-year-old student condemned to death*
OLA CAMPBELL, *Joko's mother*
AUNTY LULU, *A neighbour, the local gossip*
NEIGHBOUR, *Another woman neighbour*
PRISON DOCTOR
LOCAL PASTOR
PRISON OFFICER

ALLA GBAH

SCENE ONE

Joko Campbell, a student of about 27 years, had been tried and convicted for the murder of his mistress, Mrs Manly. Joko lies quietly in the condemned cell. He neither talks, nor sees anyone, including his mother, Mrs Ola Campbell. As the day on which he is to hang approaches, he desperately tries to understand and explains the reason for his actions without regrets.

The condemned cell. Evening. The only audible sounds are the padding of steel heels on concrete walkways. The ticking of the prison clock. Joko Campbell is having a nightmare. Joko's 'id' is personified – perhaps one of his fellow students.

STUDENT (*reproachfully*): Joko Campbell, you cannot as an intelligent, reasonable man blame anyone for the irreparable damage and misery you have brought to bear upon yourself, your mother, relatives and friends.

JOKO (*calm and bold*): I have brought no misery, no damage on anyone for which I feel guilty. Let me assure you, that I know perfectly well how precise, clear and definite a man's duty ought to be as in my case.

STUDENT (*ironically*): I don't deny the fact that you are a man.

JOKO: Who can? I am well over twenty-one.

STUDENT: I realize that fully well. But on the other hand, your claim as to having a precise, clear and definite knowledge of what a man's duty ought to be is rather freakish and groundless.

JOKO: You, no doubt, know me better than I do myself.

STUDENT: Any man, I mean any responsible intelligent man, would uphold and carry out his duties with pride and dignity – reasonably and rationally.

JOKO (*with mocked sarcasm*): Those men you are talking about belong to the great traditional institution of hypocrisy which I detest.

STUDENT: Stop being the 'Know-all' and 'End-all', Joko. The duty you claim to know so well was rash, emotional and unguarded. See where it has brought you, to the condemned cell.

JOKO: That duty changed my whole life. If it's now leading me to the gallows – it has also taught me how mysterious the impulsive feelings of love can be.

STUDENT: Has it?

JOKO: Yes. It introduced me to a life of freedom.

STUDENT: Freedom! Freedom for the hangman's noose?

JOKO: It doesn't matter one way or the other. Whether it's freedom to hang ... A freedom to be engulfed in the bosom of Mrs Manly, or alone like a hermit in a deserted island ... For me, it was a freedom which requires a beginning; and that beginning was my resolution.

STUDENT (*cold, hard*): Resolution to kill?

JOKO: Nothing in this world is done without a cause.

STUDENT: That might be true, but what is it that made you kill? (*With utmost disgust.*) Surely, it's not for such meaningless resolution and morbid freedom?

JOKO: If what you say is what you think, then I am not more intelligent or sane than those who have killed before – and those who will after me.

STUDENT: I don't understand you, Joko.

JOKO: There's a lot that cannot be understood and perceived through questions and answers.

STUDENT: Why did you quit university?

JOKO: I found it boring ... still-born ... static.

STUDENT (*thoughtfully*): Why did you run away from home? (*Pause*) Why did you run away from your mother's house? From her security, comforts ... protection?

JOKO (*with the bitterness of memory*): I had to. I was sick. Sick of her making me helpless, making me feel like a child still in the cradle, having a soother in my mouth to comfort me.

STUDENT: You are as miserable as you sound ungrateful, Joko.

JOKO: I don't care.

STUDENT: You look it. You feel it, and you do want to care. You know that, Joko. Now you are regretting it all deep down inside you.

JOKO: No, you are wrong. I had to escape before it was too late. Escape from my mother's apron strings, from her ceaseless pamperings, pattings and pettings. She and the institution of great learning purported the same tarnished ideas and ideologies – hypocrisy – stupid.

STUDENT: So, in your great escape you jumped from the old black-bottom frying-pan into the old red-hot fire?

JOKO: No. In my escape I made a discovery – but it was not as simple as you all think . . . Packing up my studies and leaving my mother's house was all my decision. My own will, not wish. Will. Believe me I have no regrets, no remorse.

STUDENT: You are despicable.

JOKO: I know I am. I also know how to take care of myself, and choose for myself. So don't start insinuating.

STUDENT: So Mrs Manly was your indisputable, immediate choice. Your mother's contemporary in age.

JOKO: Not in thoughts and feelings, thank heaven.

STUDENT: She was old enough to be your mother, and you are intelligent enough to know what that means in this society and surroundings.

JOKO: I am intelligent enough to feel. Yes! Feel that from the moment I met her . . . that very moment our body and soul fused together as one. We didn't have time for the fabricated ethics of decadent puritan society.

STUDENT: So had many other young men of your age who ignorantly and innocently fall victim to Mrs Manly and others of her type.

JOKO: Mine . . . Ours was different.

STUDENT: Different? How different? Wasn't she the 'Queen Bee' of the town? Big Sissie with 'Feather pillow bosom', chirruping from school to schoolboy, wantonly seducing them.

JOKO: Stop!

STUDENT: Enjoying new sensations . . . new blood.

JOKO: Stop! Stop! It is not fair to judge people you don't know – let alone when they are dead.

STUDENT: What happened to all the young girls in town? Did you get tired of them? What did Mrs Manly have, that girls of your age hadn't got and copiously too?

JOKO: It is sacrilegious to compare her to the world of girls who lack feelings. They are faithless, passionless, devoid of affection. She was my Madonna. That unique inexpressible beauty and love which transforms everything. That which gives life, new life, purpose and hope and meaning to the fallen.

STUDENT (*surprised*): When were you a fallen?

JOKO: I was not only a fallen. I was among the lifeless and useless. A destitute persecuted in that macabre institution of learning called a university and that moralistic cul-de-sac haven of a home. I had to escape and quick.

STUDENT: And Mrs Manly offered you cover – refuge?

JOKO: Yes. She was like me, persecuted and destitute. We were both fallen.

STUDENT: I can see you could not help falling on her springing Vono bosom, or was it on the double bed?

JOKO (*pause*): Only the fallen have use for each other. At the start we were both united and proud of the discovery.

STUDENT: Until?

JOKO: The start was only a union in anticipation.

STUDENT: Oh yes?

JOKO: She was scared of my mother and I was aware that she was nothing but the spitting image.

STUDENT: Of your mother?

JOKO: Of the very thing I was escaping from. Nevertheless, finally our anticipation became a certainty. She was the only one to whom I felt myself drawn closely to in so many ways.

STUDENT: Financially and sexually you mean?

JOKO: In every way conceivable. We were drawn closer to each other, until love revealed itself to us as the ultimate.

STUDENT (*sarcastically*): You don't say?

JOKO: Yes, the ultimate. She was my glorious possession.

STUDENT: Until you caught her making love to another man. In the same room and on the same double bed where you took pride as master and refuge from surveillance?

JOKO: That's my business. Our business.

STUDENT: It was in turn her resolution wasn't it?

JOKO: Stop. I forbid anyone to judge her.

STUDENT: It was in time her ultimate resolution and the beginning of your downfall.

JOKO: Don't! Don't judge her – anything but her.

STUDENT: Your mother pleaded with you to come home. She pleaded and begged. But you refused. You ignored your friends and relations for a disreputable old hag. Well Joko? Your mother went to the extent of making a public nuisance of herself.

JOKO: Oh, she was not alone. She had my niece and aunts. They came with bottles, tin pans, drums; all the noising paraphernalias they could get. They abused loudly and bawdily. Curses multiplied with lewd parables. Indecent scenes unimaginable were performed before my eyes and in front of Mrs Manly's house.

STUDENT: Still you chose to stay on with her, and enjoy seeing your family disgracing themselves in broad daylight, to an unforgetting gossipy neighbourhood.

JOKO: This is a free democratic independent country, isn't it? We are supposed to be civilized people aren't we? Why worry about what the neighbours think and say? After all everyone is guilty of the same crime. They only refuse to believe and accept they are.

STUDENT: Shame on you, Joko. Shame on you. What has become of those big bright ideas of yours?

JOKO: Ideas?

STUDENT: About Independence. What does it all mean to you now? Modern western civilization. Independence. What does it all mean, Joko?

JOKO: Independence is here with us, and here to stay. It's like an infant born into a world where it did not expressly ask to be born . . . into . . .

STUDENT: Stop beating about the bush.

JOKO (*persisting*): Independence and the infant are one and the same. Synonymous. Both are new. Both learning the hard facts and uneasy ways of progressive existence. To grow. To develop into maturity. It all comes, through trial and error . . . countless mistakes and failures. That is, if the begetters could join together and make the right contributions.

STUDENT: You are one of those begetters Joko. What, if any, has been your contribution?

JOKO: Contribution to what?

STUDENT: To existence, Independence, progress.

JOKO: Nil. I have extricated myself from such burdens.

STUDENT: Why?

JOKO: In the process of creating and killing.

STUDENT: What?

JOKO: Yes: I created, then killed. (*Pause.*) I was scared. Scared of making a mess of what I had not quite prepared myself to take full responsibility for.

STUDENT: So, you accept that the claim you make on having a clear, precise and definite knowledge of what a man's duty ought to be is a freak. A groundless, rash, emotional and unguarded duty.

JOKO: As a man I performed a duty of which I had a clear, precise and definite knowledge.

STUDENT (*shouting him down*): Shame on you Joko Campbell, shame on you. Western Civilisation and Independence brought to people like you, to your doorsteps, countless blessings, innumerable virginal virtues . . . yes virtues. But you Joko, you choose only the vices.

JOKO: If I am alone in my choice, it is because I appreciate the values in the vices. That means that I am different. Like a Judas, I cheat and lie and perhaps will regret. For now, I create sensation for a static society. I am the unusual surprise; the once in a while abnegator who upsets societies, established orders and systems. Yes, I dared to cross into the camps of the under-trodden dogs, the unprivileged. Here in this cell I grace their company by finding out how it feels to be within and yet without . . . to drift.

STUDENT: Your education Joko. Your education!

JOKO: What about my education?

STUDENT: What use have you made of it? Those volumes you dwelled upon day and night, turning pages backwards and forwards. Burning the late night kerosene lamp. The time, the effort and all the money spent on you Joko.

JOKO: It will all be delivered handsomely to the hangman tomorrow morning at nine o'clock.

STUDENT: Joko, please be reasonable.

JOKO: Damn! Damn! Money, education, morals, society and system does not make me a man . . . never.

STUDENT: What makes a man, Joko? What makes you a man?

JOKO: My mother did not make a man out of me.

STUDENT: You did not give her a chance. She did try.

JOKO: Ai, so she did. My father did not make me a man.

STUDENT: But he is dead, Joko.

JOKO: Not that I know of. (*With calm.*) But since you all believe so, I will not try to prove you wrong.

STUDENT: Well, if he is alive why did you not go to him instead of Mrs Manly? Why?

JOKO: If I had, what good would it have been? What difference would it have made? You all stupidly and blindly believe that he is dead. (*Laughs.*)

STUDENT: Why, what's so funny?

JOKO: Our wrong values and obnoxious priorities. Damn! My father is as alive and strong and kicking as ony other working man you care to name.

STUDENT (*still shocked*): But, but your mother says . . .

JOKO: My mother. My mother, she is a liar. An artist of deception. She knows how to protect herself from moral shame and the scandal of our society.

STUDENT: Where is your father?

JOKO: That's the million dollar secret for both my father and mother. That's the only privileged cognizance that gives me claim to being a man. Knowing that my father is alive and that I see and meet him everyday.

STUDENT: All the more why you should have no doubts to make it known to us . . . to those who have been fooled.

JOKO: It is forbidden for me to talk to my father. To address him as father. To look upon him as a father and expect him to treat me as his son. I carry my mother's maiden name. Not my real father's name. (*Coldly.*) So you see why education does not make me a man?

STUDENT: I do.

JOKO: Can you understand why civilization cannot make me a free man? Why Independence in terms of One man, One vote will never make a thing like me a happy man?

STUDENT: But why Joko? What then? If you yourself can't make you a man.

JOKO: Love, selfless love. Freedom; freedom to live, to fight and die for what is right and good and proper. Above all, happiness. Yes happiness to go on loving and being free and making others happy.

STUDENT: What you say might be true. But perhaps only for you and a few other people. It is too generalized.

JOKO (*shouts him down*): Love. True love, that's what makes me a man. Personal freedom, that's what makes me a man. Individual happiness, that's what makes me a man. It doesn't you? Does it? Well for me, these three are together the trinity of a perfect unity. Joined together, they must be in us all. In all human respectable lives. Yes, all lives.

STUDENT: Where Joko, and when did you formulate this your philosophy?

JOKO: It is not a philosophy. It is a feeling and a genuine one at that . . . And I felt it in my moments of escape. Fleeing with Mrs Manly.

STUDENT: Couldn't you, if you were more patient, less arrogant, hasty and impertinent, have discovered your perfect unity in a better atmosphere, in more proper and decent surroundings? Couldn't this your great feeling have served a more useful and fruitful purpose with someone else?

JOKO: My mother's affair with my father, out of which I was produced, did not have a pastor's privilege. My affair with Mrs Manly which brought me here was not blessed nor graced by society's blessings. I am without blessings and favour from the moment of my conception right up to the day before the moment I cease to be. So what's all the bother about? People like me do not grumble for the way things are. Mrs Manly was my ideal and I would not have changed her for all the untouched pretty-feet virgins that are unlearned about the beauty of vulgarity, and the experiences of violent passion, that love and sex demands.

STUDENT: She must have been a woman of ability. God rest her soul in peace.

JOKO: Had you said that to her when she was alive, you would have convinced her that the world still has people capable of speaking good thoughts – thoughts of forgetting and forgiving.

STUDENT: I can still do that. Not to her though, but for you.

JOKO: Thank you for the thought. But I am perfectly at ease with myself.

STUDENT: Do me a last friendly favour. Speak to them.

JOKO: Them? Who?

STUDENT: Your mother and father. Please, please.

JOKO: So that's it. I must lick up my vomit. I must stoop to the elders as tradition demands. Bow to society. Love and respect their rejecting me. I must die begging, shamefaced and ridiculed. Yes. I get it all quite clear. The wretched of the earth. The condemned must ask forgiveness not for himself but for the satisfaction of society.

STUDENT: No, Joko. You are wrong. Your mother is not society. She is a mother who deserves to be respected by her son – her only son.

JOKO: I feel sick.

STUDENT: Try, Joko. Try.

JOKO: Let me die and be forgotten.

STUDENT: It is never too late and mothers are always forgiving.

(*Sound of boots on concrete walkway.*)

PRISON OFFICER'S VOICE: Joko Campbell, you have fifteen hours to live. (*The voice echoes.*)

STUDENT: Try, dear Joko! I am sure they will understand. Try, please try.

JOKO (*dismally*): Officer! Officer! Fifteen hours to live! Officer, I want . . . I . . . want to. I'd like to see . . . to . . . talk . . . Officer! (*His voice fades away.*)

SCENE TWO

The home of Mrs Ola Campbell. A distressed and heart-broken mother in tears explaining her sorrows to a neighbour.

OLA (*her words frequently interspersed with sniffing, nose-blowing and coughs*) I warned Joko, neighbour. I tried to protect him against loose life; cautioned him about street girls. I meant well for him. It was all for his own good, when I told him to beware of coquettish worldly women. I instructed him about not choosing friends outside his own social milieu. It was as if I was psychic. I had dreamt of how they hate him in this neighbourhood. 'Choose your friends among your equal,' I said. 'Move in the right circles, with respectable men.' I went on drumming it into him. I never stopped. But it was as if they had already cast their witch spells on him not to listen to me. As if they had blinded him into the Babylon den.

NEIGHBOUR: It is like our people will say, 'the herb that tempts the appetite of a goat, always exposes the poor animal to a disgraceful diarrhoea'.

OLA: Neighbour. Neighbour, Joko didn't do it. He couldn't: I swear, he is too young to. He is a good and well-brought-up child. He is, neighbour.

NEIGHBOUR: Take suru. Make you take suru, Mama Ola.

OLA: They framed my son, neighbour. They hate him. If he had a father – (*She breaks down into very bitter tears.*) If he had . . . God.

NEIGHBOUR (*consolingly*): Mama Ola, you must not do this to yourself. It pains I know, but try to put your case to God. Let Him fight for you.

OLA: Neighbour, tell me, what must I do now? What can I do? Who can I turn to?

NEIGHBOUR: Put your case to God.

OLA (*breathless horror*): My Joko condemned to hang? Joko! Joko, my son, my baby, my one and all.

NEIGHBOUR: Go down on both knees Mama Ola, and pray to your God; call on Him, the Father, the Son and the Holy Ghost.

OLA (*petrified*): Aunty Lulu will be rejoicing at my calamity. Songs will echo my downfall and my son's disgrace. Jealous lips and tongues will spout out hate and foul air; adding more to make it all spicy and tasty. God, you see it all. You hear it all and you know well. Show me the way. Direct me in this my time of trial and tribulation. How could this happen to me? To Joko? What went wrong? Why? Oh God! Oh God!

NEIGHBOUR: I really don't see the sense in hanging. I don't . . .

OLA: God, I challenge you. You to whom I pray by day and by night, free my son, free him from the wrath of the hangman's noose. Free Joko. (*Knock on door.*)

NEIGHBOUR: Mama Ola, take suru. Take suru.

OLA: Neighbour, the green snake that crawls unrecognized among the green grass does not bite everyday and for nothing. When it strikes, its poison kills.

NEIGHBOUR: I know, Mama Ola. I know – (*A louder knock on the door.*) There is somebody at the door.

OLA: Let them go away. Tell them to leave me alone. (*Shouts.*) Leave me alone you false sympathizers. Go away from my door and laugh.

NEIGHBOUR: Mama Ola, do calm down. Calm down please.

OLA: They gather together, neighbour. They discuss how best they should laugh at me when I pass by. They incite their children to follow me and sing lewd songs after me. They have no pity, no mercy. They forget that trouble was not meant only for one person.

NEIGHBOUR: Of course not. Trouble knocks at each and every one of our doors at the most unlikely and unexpected times.

OLA: No matter what I do, neighbour, this stain of my son's tragedy; this disgrace will never rub off. Not as long as I live in this neighbourhood.

NEIGHBOUR: Mama Ola if you listen to the noise of the market you won't buy fish. So do take suru, take suru.

OLA: You are new in this neighbourhood, neighbour. I beg of you, whatever gossips and whispers you might have heard and will hear about my son and I, do take no notice of them. Don't believe, don't believe.

NEIGHBOUR: I am a different individual and a person of my own conviction Mama Ola. I listen and weigh and make my own judgements.

OLA: They are false faces all of them neighbour. Hypocrites and slanderers. They hate without feeling and malice without reason. Their jealous talks brought hostile indifferences between Joko and me. Their infamous tongues brought misunderstandings, daily petty questionings from Joko; disrespect, quarrels and lastly separation. Then, now, shame and disgrace.

NEIGHBOUR: I understand how it feels to be alone. To bring up a child without a man and to end in such unpleasantness.

OLA: They have poisoned his mind so much against me that he has since his trial refused to see me. Refused to see me, his own mother. God, what a vicious world we live in.

NEIGHBOUR: Maybe he wants to see you but he just can't get himself to face up to it at this last minute.

OLA: I want to see my son. I want to.

NEIGHBOUR: If his father was alive it would have made all the difference.

OLA: I don't know, neighbour. (*Resigned.*) I honestly don't know. (*Door opens. Pastor enters.*)

PASTOR (*sermonizing*): When trouble weighs us down and sorrow hangs on to us like a fevered scarlet, we despairingly sink into melancholic distress, thinking and feeling that all the world has conglomerated against us and has unanimously agreed to spare us neither peace nor rest.

OLA (*restrained*): You come at last, Pastor.

PASTOR: Mrs Campbell, you ignored my knock on your door. I patiently waited for you to let me in. At least to see who it was knocking. You were intent on wanting whoever it was out there, to hear what you have to say about the people of the neighbourhood, what you think they think about you and Joko. You are wrong. Very wrong. Even if you think you are right in thinking and believing what you were saying, why don't you think that your God at this moment is not laughing at you.

OLA: Pastor, I am looking for help to save my son from the hungry gallows; from the hangman's wrath. I believe he can be saved. He is innocent. He is too young to die. Too young to die . . .

PASTOR: Let the Lord hear your prayer. He alone at this time and hour can make a just decision.

OLA: But Pastor you have known your . . . Joko since he was a boy. (*She breaks down.*)

PASTOR: Let us say a prayer. A little prayer for the boy. (*Prays.*) It is truly meet and just, that we should always and in all places give thanks to thee O God, Father Almighty, eternal God. In thee the hope of a blessed resurrection is shown to us, that they who are saddened by the certain necessity of dying be comforted by the promise of eternal life. We believe O Lord, that the life of the faithful is changed, not taken away; that the abode of this earthly sojourn being dissolved, an eternal dwelling is prepared in heaven. Where thy Angels, Archangels and Saints await us and with all the heavenly hosts with thee who liveth and reigneth, world without end.

NEIGHBOUR: Amen. Thy will be done.

OLA: Thank you, Pastor. Thank you ever so much. May the good Lord hear our prayer.

NEIGHBOUR (*sighs*): I am going now Mama Ola, but I will call by later. Goodbye, Pastor.

PASTOR: Goodbye and God bless.

NEIGHBOUR (*as she goes*): Take suru oh, Mama Ola. Do I beg, make you take suru. (*Door closes behind her.*)

OLA: I did not expect you would come Pastor. I thought you had so much preaching to do with your growing flock.

PASTOR: I have come to ask you to come with me.

OLA: Come with you where, are you out of your mind?

PASTOR: The quicker you pull yourself together, the better it will be.

OLA: You should have thought of that twenty-eight years ago. I would have realized my station in life and would perhaps have not got into this degrading spectacle.

PASTOR: You will be letting yourself into greater scandal and disgrace by breaking the oath we took and the allegiance of secrecy we swore together to keep until we die.

OLA (*with rage*): What does it matter? Allegiance, Oath, death. What does it all mean any more?

PASTOR: Quiet now, Ola. Don't shout or you will be helping your enemies to jest. Keep your head up. Pride, my dear. Never fall below your station in life. The honour you deserve will come soon to you, I promise. I am as worried and as unhappy over the turn of events that the hand fate has so wilfully played us. Yet we must be of good courage. Cheer up and let's not waste more time. The child would like to talk to us both. He needs us. We must not let him down.

OLA: Stop.

PASTOR: The laws of man are too complicated. I have never tried to understand its mechanics. I don't think its makers themselves do.

OLA: You never will because you have secured yourself in the firm concrete of the establishment. You are safe all the way. From here to eternity. Safe as the moon in the sky.

PASTOR: Let's go.

OLA: Let this be the last time you ever come my way.

PASTOR: I will remember, I promise you. (*As they close door behind them, we hear Ola singing. For music see p. 74.*)

OLA (*singing, the Pastor joins in the refrain*):
There will be no sickness in heaven
There will be no night there
There will be no dying in heaven
There will be no night there
There will be no hatred in heaven
There will be no night there
There will be no parting in heaven
There will be no night there
There will be no hanging in heaven

There will be no night there
There will be no night there

SCENE THREE

Fade into a street atmosphere. Footsteps padding and lazily shuffling. Various noises of cars and carts. Bicycles belling. A guitarist is playing and singing. The song is picked up by passers by and children. Rather satirical and topical. For music see p. 75.

GUITARIST:
Tranga yaase nor good oh
tranga yaase nor good oh
if you falla big-sisi
rope go eat you wase
you go fen you sef nar crux

Joko Campbell runaway nar 'ouse
Joko Campbell runaway nar college
when di whole country begin look for 'am
den fen am big 'oman pallar *(laughter in-between)*

Tranga yaase nor good oh
tranga yaase nor good oh
when you werr big man trussis
wrapala wit' big 'oman
you go end nar Carlington

Joko Campbell don krais for Mrs Manly
Mrs Manly dat sabie how for bahyo-bahyo
Foofoo chop en satida effor di compel
turn Joko loos en mass 'im mole

Tranga yaase nor good oh
tranga yaase nor good oh
if you falla big-sisi
rope go eat you wase
you go fen you sef nar crux

Joko Campbell nar you fen am for you sef
nar you wan know how di 'sweet-sweet' tase'
titty lek en bor-bor love, nar im dat
big 'oman lappa, nor to pekin play 'grun

Tranga yaase nor good oh
tranga yaase nor good oh
when you werr big man trussis
en wrapala wit big-'oman yarasa
you go disgrace lek chek-chek foll (*Fade into.*)

NEIGHBOUR: Aunty Lulu! (*Calls louder.*) Aunty Lulu!

AUNTY LULU: Neighbour how are you? Come and let me
see you. How is everything neighbour? I have jes' been
saying to myself whether you will be spendin' the whole
day wit Mrs Campbell. How do you fin' her?

NEIGHBOUR: I was only there to give my own little moral
support as I expect all good neighbours should.

LULU: You think say if it was you in trouble dat woman
would lift one eyebrow. You have time to waste . . .

NEIGHBOUR: I pity her, neighbour.

LULU: We should do more than you. But we don't. She
deserves what she's getting. She make her own bed of
thorns, let her manage it herself.

NEIGHBOUR: Why do you say such hard things?

LULU: Because her Joko child was the never-do-wrong type.
The always clever, doing the right things in the eyes of
the mother. That brat was a terror. He was always ready
to curse a ghost and fight the devil. He had no respect and
showed none for any of us. He bullied the little ones when
he was not corrupting them. He was a misfit in this
neighbourhood and you dare say it for his mother to hear;
she'll tell you how to find your way back into you mother's
womb.

NEIGHBOUR; I suppose all mothers are like that. But they
really mean no harm.

LULU: You are new in this neighbourhood, neighbour.

C

Thank God you come at a time when we have been relieved of the evil hunting spirit that spared us neither peace nor rest, day and night. Come rain or sun or harmattan.

NEIGHBOUR: It sounds terrifying.

LULU: Thank God, Joko is going to hang. We hope that his end will frighten the life out of his many followers in the neighbourhood.

NEIGHBOUR: Was Joko all that influentially wicked?

LULU: Wicked? He was a dreadful monster. Once he accused pastor George of taking bribes. He was daring enough to call the pastor to his face, a 'dirty old dog collar'.

NEIGHBOUR: Why? There must be some unexplained reason.

LULU: Bad upbringing if you ask me. Oh yes. Oh yes. In fact, just before you moved into the neighbourhood, Joko and his gang, lawless ones, went about talking infamy about the pastor.

NEIGHBOUR: But why the pastor and not somebody else?

LULU: I wouldn't know, but, eh (*scrapes her throat*) come and sit down, neighbour. Rumour has it – don't say that I told you – they rumour that pastor is Joko's father. True or false it's none of my business. Well Ola was a promiscuous one in her younger days you know.

NEIGHBOUR: Oh yes?

LULU: That's why they say it is Ola who puts Joko up against the pastor. Poor man, just recently there was rumour that he visits his female church members – some mind you – different days of the week after their husbands have gone to work. What for, I wouldn't know. Would you, neighbour?

NEIGHBOUR: No, Aunty Lulu. I wouldn't like to think.

LULU: Well, they say he is very seductive. Mind you he is very handsome and with such a charming angelic voice, I wouldn't underestimate the wolf in sheep's clothing.

NEIGHBOUR: Tell me more, Aunty Lulu.

LULU: You will find out in time. As for now, Joko's cup has run over and it is no surprise to those of us who knew the kind of character the boy had in him. That he should end up in this way, was long coming to him. My grandmother use to say to us; if you play with God, Jesus Christ will make you shit. (*Laughs.*)

NEIGHBOUR (*sighs heavily*): I pity Mama Ola.

LULU (*shocked*): Pity her? What for? (*With spite*) She is only reaping the fruits from the seeds she sowed. Didn't you hear what she shouted in court when the death sentence was passed? (*Imitating.*) 'My son didn't do it. Joko is innocent.' Innocent be damned. I am so happy, so relieved that we have laws and a few people left in our courts that will not become corrupt. It is only they who can protect us from such an indulgent dangerous mother and such wayward aggressive sons.

NEIGHBOUR: How do you think this will affect Mama Ola's life in the neighbourhood?

LULU: It bothers me not one bit. Not a stitch.

NEIGHBOUR: I can't help feeling sorry for her.

LULU: If you ask my advice, don't keep her company. Tomorrow by this time Joko will be dead and we will have no more cause to worry of any Jack the raper. His candle will be blown and blotted out of the neighbourhood for ever.

NEIGHBOUR (*teasing*): His ghost will hunt, if he was unjustly punished.

LULU: It will not. We are going down to that prison to laugh away his ghost and perform the ceremony that will silence body, soul and spirit. Not even his smell will be remembered.

NEIGHBOUR: I will be there too.

LULU: Come with us.

NEIGHBOUR: No. I am going alone. I want to be alone.

LULU: You mean you are going to mourn with Ola?

NEIGHBOUR: No I am going to protest.

LULU (*with horror*): What?

NEIGHBOUR: Yes. I am going to protest. I do not know Joko. I don't side with what he has done to anybody that was bad. I think it was evil of him to kill. But I cannot judge him, since, as I say, I don't know him. But I have to protest because I am one of those queer mixed-up people, as some people will call me. I, in my own way, resent hanging. This capital punishment belongs to the decadent, distant, ruthless generations of the past. I am a reformer, Aunty Lulu. I believe that Joko needs help. Your help and my help and everybody's help in this neighbourhood. It was up to you all to have helped him into making a decent and better citizen. Your interest in him would have helped to reassure him. To cure his mind's malady.

LULU (*absentmindedly*): What did you say?

NEIGHBOUR: His sickness, Aunty Lulu. Joko is sick in the head.

LULU: Not only him. His mother too.

NEIGHBOUR: A long prison sentence might, together with – what they call it – a psychiatric treatment have helped him greatly.

LULU: And the mother?

NEIGHBOUR: She is harmless.

LULU (*as if bitten by a viper*): Harmless?

NEIGHBOUR (*with irony*): Yes, harmless. If she is left alone and not bothered by petty squabbles about what is right and what is wrong from people who know no better.

LULU (*sharply*): What exactly do you mean, neighbour?

NEIGHBOUR (*with indignation, full of sarcasm*): What I said, people like to take a spade to shovel the mote out of their neighbours' eyes.

LULU: I put my own house first in order, neighbour. I do not interfere with, nor poke my nose into people's business.

NEIGHBOUR: What is it that is eating you up inside, Aunty Lulu? Why do some of you talk with hate about Joko and Mama Ola, why?

LULU (*warning tone of anger*): Be careful of what you say, neighbour. I warn you for your own sake. Be very, very careful.

NEIGHBOUR (*coldly*): Why is it that most of you find it so much of a rejoicing at the uneventful turn fate has taken on them? Why?

LULU: You surprise me, neighbour.

NEIGHBOUR: Not as much as you do me.

LULU (*sarcastically*): Yes?

NEIGHBOUR: You will have a good rejoicing tomorrow, I hope?

LULU: I will not be alone.

NEIGHBOUR (*pointedly*): Then on Sunday, you will all go to church and pray, 'Father forgive us our trespasses as we forgive them that trespass against us'.

LULU (*getting hot*): Did you come to my house to abuse me? Did Ola ask you to come abuse me?

NEIGHBOUR: She is not that type of person. She is more decent than you make her to be.

LULU: You are trying to make trouble for yourself. You will get trouble if it is trouble you want I promise you.

NEIGHBOUR: What a character hypocrite you all are. If God was as evil as you all, he would strike down the whole lot of you; shameless bunch of no-do-good idiots. (*She goes leaving Lulu raging.*)

LULU (*raging*): You call me hypocrite? You come into my house and abuse me. We have a bone to pick, me and you. You will tell me where you were when Joko and his mother were giving me hell. Were you here when they abelled me a lopsided gate? When Joko was invoking my ldead ancestors with curses, where were you? Why do you have to come here and take sides, why? Who be you god-mother from nowhere, who be you? Well, you have come into the right church, but squat on the wrong pew. I will teach you your place. You just wait. Just you wait. I will let you know me by name. Just you wait.

(*General footsteps as in the beginning of the scene. For music see p. 76.*)

GUITARIST:
Ah shame Joko
Ah shame oh
Ah shame Joko
Ah shame oh
We bin yeri say
nar you good pass wee
but now 'E look lek say
you nar sarra fell

Tell all di land Joko is to hang
Joko Campbell is a murderer
Tell all di land how he killed di gal
Joko Campbell, squeeze and squeeze her throat

We shame Joko
we shame oh
we shame Joko
we shame oh
you mama bin say
how you go be great
but now 'E look lek say
da jiwnie nor take

Tell all di land how Joko use for brag
Joko Campbell bin too good for we
Tell all di land, nar bin big bully
Joko Campbell, nor sabie for 'fraid

We shame Joko
we shame oh
we shame Joko
we shame oh
when we yerri say
you da insie da

we all know now say
you werr am lek maskita boot.

SCENE FOUR

(*The prison cell. Boot strides on walkway.*)

OFFICER: Joko Campbell, you have thirteen more hours to live.

JOKO (*jokingly*): Officer, how do you bury murderers?

OFFICER: I haven't the faintest idea.

JOKO: Has this prison an undertaker?

OFFICER: Not to my knowledge.

JOKO: What about experienced grave-diggers?

OFFICER: I will try to find out for you if you think it is of absolute importance.

JOKO: Who writes the epitaphs?

OFFICER: I will have to make a note of finding that out as well if you are very concerned.

(*Footsteps come nearer.*)

JOKO: Who is coming Officer?

OFFICER: The doctor and a pastor.

JOKO: I see.

OFFICER: I suppose they are the people you asked to see.

JOKO: I did. Did I? When?

OFFICER: Well, If you didn't they must have requested to see you since they are coming to the death row.

PASTOR (*as they approach*): How are you today, Joko?

JOKO (*cold and detached*): My soul is perfectly alright pastor.

DOCTOR (*jokes*): And your body?

JOKO: Physically fit and strong. (*Cynically.*) My mind of course is mentally balanced. All in all doctor, I am sober and well capable. Fit and ready to swing in the morning.

DOCTOR: You have not been eating.

JOKO: Man does not live by bread alone. Isn't that right pastor?

PASTOR: Quite right, Joko. Quite right indeed.

JOKO: Am very glad you support me for the first time, Pastor.

DOCTOR: We are also pleased that you've decided to see Pastor and talk also with your mother.

JOKO: But I didn't. I don't wish to. Not now or ever.

PASTOR: It will put her mind at ease, Joko.

JOKO: And your's, Pastor?

PASTOR: There is nothing like the peace of mind which passeth all understanding.

JOKO: Another of your outwitting little nasty schemes, eh? Now, Pastor, I have helped you to lead a decent normal life in a decent schemising society. Don't try to upset me at this very last minute. Go away with your peace of unnatural understanding.

DOCTOR: It would help if you try to get it all out of you, Joko.

JOKO: Get what all out?

DOCTOR: The bitterness. Frustration and – you know. It is all in you there somewhere. Say it all and . . . well, just tell the pastor, he will understand.

JOKO: That's a foregone conclusion. Me and the pastor are like a cat and a dog. We hate each other. We know why. It is impossible for him to understand or help me. It is a betrayal to my pride, my manhood to look upon him for anything worthy of any decent human being . . .

DOCTOR (*gasps*): Joko!

JOKO: The pastor is well aware of what I am saying. Isn't that so, Pastor?

PASTOR: Will you continue to be difficult, Joko, even at a time like this?

JOKO: Since you have taken it upon yourselves to come and disturb the living dead, let me ask you two – you who are friends of the rich and the poor, you who scout with the influential and indulge nonentities, you who profess to understand the sane and insane, to love the old and the young, to respect the literate and illiterate and to be able to communicate with both the living and the dead.

PASTOR: What, Joko?

JOKO (*ignores him*): I ask you both. Can you befriend a murderer? Can you take a murderer in confidence and protect him?

DOCTOR (*stammers*): I . . . I . . . would.

JOKO: You don't have to stammer, Doctor. You don't have to answer because it is not all that important. But think on it when I am gone.

PASTOR (*catching his breath*): We are all important in the sight of God, Joko.

JOKO: But not equally represented in the sight and minds and opinions of some people.

DOCTOR: I see what you mean, Joko.

JOKO: Do you, Doctor? Both of you are men of class. Status. You are symbols of great attractions; and command respect 'unto whom all blessings flow'.

DOCTOR: How do you mean?

JOKO: You are men of reputable professions. The two professions from which our society seems to be taking its cue. You, Pastor, you enrich the soul. You supply the vacuum of salvation. You whet the appetites of human quest and longing for eternal life in the heavenly kingdom at the right hand of God. In simple words, they believe when you tell them there is a place for them in heaven. And you, Doctor. The great physician. The body mechanic. The man with the magic-wand. With your stethoscope, you can tell the symptoms of maladies to come. Diagnose, cure and prescribe life assurances. You give hope and courage. Together you restore great faith. Now, can you together undertake to cure the inexpressible feelings of unverbalized love? Can you make the same resolutions I made?

PASTOR: Resolutions do not always justify the means to their determination. Nor do they always produce effective results. There should be more to it than just mere rationalization of hit or miss. You were on the line of beginning the life of a true Christian who questions his faith; but your love attitude was immoral.

JOKO: You sound like a hawk, Pastor.

DOCTOR (*reproaching him*): Joko.

JOKO: I am a fallen man, Doctor. I have nothing to gain or lose whether I misbehave; and with Pastor I have nothing to gain or to expect.

PASTOR (*coughs*): I'd rather leave than get you all upset and worked up.

JOKO: You came especially for that, Pastor. To get me upset. You also brought my mother to get me worked up. You brought the doctor to see how I would react. You left my mother somewhere around to listen before she will make her dramatic entrance.

PASTOR: You have it all wrong.

JOKO: Like always. I am still never right.

PASTOR: I didn't say that.

JOKO: What you say doesn't matter any more. It has never mattered before. Tomorrow by this time I will be dead. I suppose you feel it your duty to pay me your last tribute by your presence. Not grace.

PASTOR: Death for us all, Joko, is inevitable.

JOKO: Some of us go sooner than others. Some like me choose the way it should be . . . (*Pastor scrapes his throat.*) Rather I help society by tempting it to help me make an easy early choice.

DOCTOR: I think it is about time you see your mother.

JOKO: Not yet Doctor. Besides, I do not particularly wish to see the woman. Now, Pastor, if you were in my place behind these iron bars, would you worry?

PASTOR: God knows. I . . . I . . .

JOKO: Would you, Doctor?

DOCTOR: Depends.

JOKO: Would you be scared?

DOCTOR: Might be.

JOKO: What would you have been thinking about?

PASTOR: That's very critical.

JOKO: Doctor, would you have given outward reactions to a nagging, bugging, pricking conscience?

PASTOR: People react differently, Joko. In such a situation awake or asleep, it is your subconscious that is at work because without a strong will power madness is never distant.

JOKO: I knew you would come out with something whitewash like that Pastor. Just like you reacted cold to me years ago when I called you 'dirty old dog collar'.

DOCTOR: Joko.

PASTOR: That, Joko, was your mother's responsibility.

JOKO: Yes. Well said, Pastor. You have finally helped me to prepare my soul to meet my God. I didn't call you here. But you came. Why? Did you think I wanted peace of mind? Do you think your holy presence is necessary? No. For me the silence of the prison officers; those detached voices telling me the time I have left; their steel boots on concrete; these dead unspeaking walls and all its concrete tensions have helped me through the agony of finding peace within myself.

OFFICER: Joko Campbell, you have twelve more hours to live.

JOKO: That, only the voice instils fear and arouses tension of scare. It also tempts speech from what is already dead.

DOCTOR: You should rest, Joko.

JOKO: Rest, Doctor, is for the weary. Not for me. (*Footsteps approaching.*) Rest at this time when I hear my mother's footsteps approaching? No.

PASTOR: Joko, please?

JOKO: Pastor you amuse me. You know, you sound a little cautioned. Is it a warning for me to be of good cheer, Pastor? Or just that we should not talk of the past?

PASTOR: Be sensible.

JOKO: As you are tactful, Pastor?

PASTOR: Try not to hurt yourself by trying to hurt her.

JOKO: No, Pastor, I will not hurt her. Nor you, either. Not when I know how much you gave up, everything, even your own flesh and blood, to remain married to your wife and your gospel according to decent moralized society.

PASTOR: What are you trying to dig up now?

JOKO: The truth. My father.

DOCTOR (*shocked*): What did you say, Joko?

PASTOR: My dear boy, your mind is very confused.

JOKO: My mind is not confused. Accept the truth for once in the presence of an outsider. Accept, father.

PASTOR: It must be very trying to be going through such distressing mental and physical torture.

JOKO: I have been going through it for the last twenty-seven years. A long time wouldn't you agree? Why did you deny me, father? Was it my fault or was it something to do with Mother?

OLA (*approaches trying to suppress her tears*): Joko, Joko. My son, my one and only.

JOKO: You've come at the right time, Mother; and it's good to see you with Father at a time like this. It proves that you two did, in the first place, agree to have a child. Why was I rejected when I was born, Mother? (*Pause.*) You see, Doc, they go quiet. No sigh. No tears. No words. I am of their sperm. Their handywork. Is that not so Mother? Father (*Pause.*) Quietness in itself is guilt. Speechlessness ranks closely with shame. That's what your good society is full of – ashamed people. Guilty people. People full of hidden regrets. Afraid that their sin and crimes will give way to fears of passions of the past.

DOCTOR: This is embarrassing.

JOKO: I lived, Doctor, like an unwanted child. I grew up a lost cause. End up here as a condemned man. A product of two people's whimsical fancies. Society's figure of fun.

OLA: Stop! Stop, Joko. Stop!

JOKO: So you see, Doc, it does hurt somewhere not to be able to have a decent past. It pains some people to have a tarnished present and it pleases others to have to live up to their reputation at the expense of another's destruction.

DOCTOR: And you think they are responsible for your ending where you are now?

JOKO: I would not blame my fate on their folly. Yet I cannot help remembering how beautifully sick I felt when my mother told me the story of the 'little rascal' and then followed it up by pointing out my father to me as he stood gallantly and gracefully, all innocent on that rainy Sunday morning on the pulpit preaching to us: 'Do unto others as you would they should do unto you . . .' Remember, Mother.

OLA (*choked*): Yes, Joko.

JOKO: The little boy was to be destroyed by wild animals in his father's forest. The father was an old jealous king. 'A proud king'. 'A good king'. 'He loved his people and was proud he alone understood them'. Isn't that so, Mother? (*She sobs. Joko continues.*) Well the king wanted to make a great sacrifice. In doing so, he could make the people happy all of the time.

DOCTOR: Was he robbing Peter to pay Paul?

JOKO: Something like that. Wouldn't you agree, Father?

OLA: Stop Joko. This disgrace, I can't bear it any further.

JOKO: Father wanted it this way, Mother. He planned it all before he invited you here. Now, Doc, you are going to be the only living witness to this well kept secret between my mother and her good old pal, Pastor George, my father. Doesn't he look holy, Doctor? With the face of a Pope; the voice of an angel and his words as tender and gentle as the petals of roses in spring. But his heart? I wonder what that looks like. Can you guess?

DOCTOR: I think you must go, Pastor, and Mrs Campbell.

JOKO: Before you go, Mother, I want to tell you something.

OLA: What, Joko?

JOKO: Try to dip into the scanty past of your historic life. Try putting it together with your present achievements; maybe you might perhaps come to formulate your own ideas which will lead you to take the first thinking towards making a resolution. Maybe it will then help you, to help those like you, to find out why and how they tick. You might discover what makes you a woman.

OLA (*going towards him*): Joko you have killed everything in me. You have not forgiven me, my son. I did what I did for your own good fortune. I did not expect it to have gone this way.

JOKO: Like a sheep some of us allow ourselves to be led and be misled.

OLA: I love you, my son. Believe me, I will always love you.

JOKO: 'Some love too little and some too late.'
'Some sell and others buy; some do the deed with many a tear and some without a sigh; For each man kills the thing he loves yet each man does not die.'

DOCTOR: That sounds like something I've read.

OLA (*bursts out crying*): Joko, why do you have to die?

JOKO: Because I killed, Mother. Hard and cold. I killed. Tell it to your congregation on Sunday, Pastor, and tell them also that I am not one bit sorry.

OLA: Joko, my child, my little only one.

JOKO (*luringly*): Come closer, Mother. I want to tell you a secret that you will share with everyone when I am dead. You will keep it in remembrance of me.

OLA: Yes, Joko, anything that will make you happy.

JOKO: Come closer, Mother. Bring your ear closer and listen very carefully, Mother. (*She bends her right ear to him. With all his strength he bites it off with a grunt.* OLA *screams, running away as fast as she could like a being possessed and mad. Screaming and shouting inaudibly.*)

OLA: Help. Help. He bit off my ear. Help! Mercy, God, mercy. Jesus come to my rescue. Come, oh come and see me disgrace and shame. Come, help, help. My ear.

PASTOR (*in shock and rage*): Good God, you are far gone mad.

DOCTOR: How could you, Joko? How could you? (*Rushes after Mrs Campbell.*)

JOKO: That, Doctor, was the anti-climax of the 'little rascal' left to be destroyed by wild animals. He did not ask to be born. Why should he suffer alone for crimes he did not intend to commit? Why?

PASTOR: You have no soul. No salvation.

JOKO (*shouts after her*): Go with that in remembrance of me, Mother.

PASTOR: You are mad. Mad. Mad.

JOKO: Think what you may as much as it pleases you to think so. It might help your appetite tonight or maybe tomorrow after you are sure I am no more to bring you to justice; to expose you to a public that is always ready to take revenge for revenge sake, and destroy what is not theirs, and bears no relationship to them.

PASTOR: You are mad, Joko. Mad.

JOKO: And in your opinion, I am better off dead. Yes?

PASTOR: You are an evil omen and a curse to society.

JOKO: And a threat to you.

PASTOR: You are beyond redemption.

JOKO: Go, Father. Go and preach the gospel. Go now, society needs your type. Go tell them that the devil is evil. tell them to run away from all those things that are black looking. Go and leave me alone. I am black and I love the way I am. Simple and plain black.

PASTOR: May the Lord have mercy on your unrepenting soul.

JOKO: Hypocrite! Stop casting your meaningless priceless pearls on a black swine. Dirty old dog collar! (*Pastor walks away. Pause. A definite stride of steel heel boots approaches. The clock strikes eight alternating with the strides. On the last stroke of eight another step, then stop. A metallic voice booms out with excruciating poignancy.*

PRISON OFFICER'S VOICE: Joko Campbell. (*Echoes.*) Joko

Campbell you have one more, last hour to live. Sixty more minutes to live . . . (*Joko bursts out laughing as the voice echoes. His laughter gets more and more hysterical, echoing all around. It goes on and on, until the clock begins to strike nine o'clock. His laughing more hysterical. Finally he breaks down to a frightened cry and calls . . .*)

JOKO (*distant*): Mother. Mother. (*Fading in wailing tears.*) Mother. I need you mother. (*Fades out.*)

There will be no sick-ness in hea-ven

There will be no night there

2nd verse: There will be no dy-ing in hea-ven
There will be no night there   (and so on).

1st. verse

Tra- nga yaase not good oh

tra- nga yaase not good oh

If you fala big- si si rope go eat you wase

you go fen you sef nar crux

Jo- ko Campbell run- away nar 'ouse

Jo- ko Campbell run- away co- lle- ge

when di whole country be- gin look for 'am

den fen am big 'om man pa- llar

Alla Gbah

1st. verse

Ah shame Jo- ko   Ah shame oh

Ah shame Jo- ko   Ah shame oh

We bin ye- ri   say

nar you good pass wee

but now 'E look lek say

you nar sa- rra fell

Tell all di land   Jo- ko   is to hang
Tell all di land   how he killed di gal

Jo- ko Campbell is ·a   mur- der- er
Jo- ko Campbell squeeze and squeeze her throat

Gbana-Bendu

CHARACTERS

BEGGAR, *A tramp. Also first drunk*

SHADOW, *A tramp. Also second drunk*

GBAKANDAS, *Society men. (Night burglars and followers of Ur'* *Tamrokoh)*

UMU, *An uninitiated virgin*

UR'TAMROKOH, *The mouthpiece of Gbakanda's gods. A super-* *stitious priest*

MAMMY-QUEEN, *Gbakanda woman. Palm-wine trader*

PO-JOE, *Umu's father*

Chorus of Gbakanda women

Bush spirits dressed in leaves and skins and tree-bark

GLOSSARY

Gbana-Bendu (*p. 77*): strong or great 'Bendu' (Bendu means a ruler).

Gbakanda (*p. 77*): could mean strength, but does not necessarily have to be. Fearlessness. Determined people.

Ojeh (*p. 81*): Secret Society known among West African people, especially in big cities. Members of this cult are generally pseudo-affluent.

Kan-Kan-Doma-Doma (*p. 81*): an expression of excitement.

Yaegaydugi (*p. 81*): an expression intoning sarcasm.

Okpolor-Jabone (*p.81*): a frog's jaw-bone (Sarcasm).

Doombuleku (*p. 82*): expressing insipidity. Morbid.

Whayraekpae Fangay (*p. 82*): a concoction of dried potent herbs mixed with granulated broken bottle which when blown, sprinkled, sprayed or thrown at someone, makes the person itch and the skin irritable.

Orbeita Attefoh (*p. 82*): green leaved vegetables which when cooked as sauce or relish, sometimes concocted as a potential 'Medicine for love'.

Ordonyor (*p. 82*): A fool.

Orgorrawdor (*p. 82*): oblong head.

Okobo-Manja (*p. 82*): a great eunuch.

'*Look how 'E da twis' en turn,*' etc. (*p. 82*): see how he turns and turns and turns, etc.

Sally-wan-sie (*p. 83*): marionette.

Hawujor (*p. 85*): a ritual feast for the dead.

Komorjade (*p. 85*): a ritual feast for child's circumcision.

Krais (*p. 85*): madness.

Sharowyae (*ing*) (*p. 86*): unnecessary talking and explaining.

Poda-Poda (*p. 87*): Mini-bus service. (Not owned by Government.)

Min 'em ba'kor (*p. 89*): it is mine.

Ur' yaem ong (*p. 89*): liar: you're lying.

Ur' yaem 'ong min 'em ba kur (*p. 89*): you're lying. It's mine.

Krifi Sarra (*p. 91*): sacrifice to Krifi.

Oku (*p. 93*): death.

Koboko (*p. 94*): a whip of ill omen. Used to destroy. It is believed that the koboko used on men, makes them become impotent.

Alaki-Perkin (*p. 94*): child of curse.

Tranga yaase (*p. 94*): hard headedness. Stubborn.

Watin (*p. 94*): like what.

lék (*p. 94*): like or just affection premature.

you sef (*p. 94*): your self.

Gbana whey nar 'im you da look for (*p. 94*): Gbana that you are looking for.

We sef lek am (*p. 94*): we also do like him.

Gbana whey you marrade to (*p. 95*): Gbana that you are married to, etc.

Akpata (*p. 96*): a flat rock.

Mumu (*p. 96*). Dumb one.

Fape (*p. 97*): finished. Wipe away.

Borfima (*p. 98*): curing charm. Charm of good luck for success. Usually made out of various human parts, such as the genitals, human blood, etc.

Lasmany (*p. 98*): a liquid. Could be good or bad as intended by the herbalist. Most times used for drinking and rubbing. Its effectiveness most times depends on what purpose it is intended for. It is poisonous to rub Lasmamy that is intended for drinking. Vice versa.

Mundoh (*p. 102*): grabbing a big mouthful with the hand.

Yan-Ka-Die (*p. 105*): peace is here.

Dorballeh (*p. 106*): pay respects. Obeisance.

Bondo-Bush (*p. 110*): most important and highly respectable indigenous woman's secret society in Sierra Leone.

Akpeteshe (*p. 116*): home-made illicit gin.

Ogeri-Kanday (*p. 117*): awfully disgusting smell.

Gbarra (*p. 117*): interfere. Take up other people's case.

Foroku (*p. 117*): completely disgraced and extinguished.

Butu-me-look (*p. 117*): stoop down and I'll look at you from 'Under'.

Skammish (*p. 117*): break into pieces.

Jabbat (*p. 117*): indecent mouthing or talking.

Yorror mouth (*p. 118*): scum mouth.

Chun-chun-naam-paelae (*p. 120*): expression and rhythm of drunks.

Wahala (*p. 120*): unnecessary trouble.

Wonko-wan-yie (*p. 121*): demented short-sighted evil person. (Evil looking.)

Wan-foot-Jombie (*p. 121*): an evil spirit that hunts at night. It is said to have one wooden leg and miles away its wooden legged thudding can be heard. It is so fearful that none dare go out or sleep while it is around.

Tonko-Baelae (*p. 131*): tongue-twister. Satirical name for rogues and immature diplomats.

Yanda-Yanda (*p. 138*): over there. Quite a distance.

Ronko (*p. 153*): a special society gown. Worn only by those who belong to that particular society. (In this case Ur 'Tamrokoh and the Gbakanda men.)

GBANA-BENDU

ACT ONE: SCENE ONE

*Early dawn. A deserted typical African untarred roadside. In the
background is an unidentifiable mud-hut and shanty village – imit-
ated, Victorian architecture – faintly reminiscent of early 1900–
1912 settlements somewhere in West Africa.*

*The setting throughout the play should suggest the tawdry and
corrupting influence of the West – a spoilt rather than an unspoilt
Africa. As it stands at the moment it contradicts itself.*

*Shadow is a small fellow in bright, rough-sewn African clothes
which are not too well fitting; a little skull cap; pair of gym shoes
which are torn and dirty. At rise of curtain two men are on stage,
one, Shadow, is trying out mock-acrobatics, leaping, and standing
on his head, walking with his hands and finally doing strong 'Ojeh'
dance, singing to himself, the other beggar is fast asleep.*

SHADOW: Kan-kan . . . doma-doma, Kan-kan . . . doma-
doma, Kan-kan . . . (*He yells with shrill excitement.*) Yaegaydugi! Okpolor. Jabone. (*Points to Beggar who is fast asleep.*)
Some people are born shameless. Look at him. Curse upon
curse upon curse heaped on his head. He has his mother's
curse on his head . . . his father's spit in his eyes . . . his
elders' tongue-twisted curse-words behind him . . . his
children's declamation . . . and not to mention his wife's
daily prayer, that God should destroy him like he had
done no other man who ever looked upon a woman's
face and left her to suffer without a penny, a house, except
with children and debt upon debt. Oh, my friend, you are a
doomed clawless leopard. I pity you lame lion though once
a mighty-mouthy hunter. I pity your condition. (*He
laughs heartily. Settles himself down. He begins to pull the hairs
off his head singly and forcefully. He sings to himself.*) Kan-kan,
doma-doma, kan-kan, doma-doma. Kan-kan, doma-doma.
(*He makes sure that he collects the hairs in the other hand after
careful scrutinization. Pensively.*) Yaegaydugi. Cats eyes do

change size. Our world spells 'Itself' destructive. Some
people who look like people. Think they hear people callin'
them 'People', expertise in dilly-dally full hardy. In sleep
they funky-dilly-dally. Awake, they cooly-dilly-dally-bully-
dawdle with the times. With people all the time. (*Gets up.*)
Empty plate lying unused in a dilapidated ruin castle
kitchen. (*Points to Beggar.*) Like him: Doombuleku, over
there. (*Dances over to him.*) Kan-kan, doma-doma, kan-kan,
doma-doma, kan-kan, doma-doma, kan-kan, doma-
doma. (*Shouts.*) Hail Master! He believes he has complete power over the world of Misfits which he intends
to blast. (*Beggar turns on his other side.*) Hail: peace be
unto you sah. (*Beggar turns again.*) Look how 'E da twist
an' turn leke for say 'E get whayraekpae nar 'im body.
(*Laughs.*) 'Im sleep wan O' 'E drunk. Awake O, that worse.
He jes leke person whey every one fit wipe their han' an'
mou't 'pon after dey finish eat big-big foofoo chop wit'
orbeita. Kan-kan, doma-doma. Kan-kan. doma-doma,
Kan-kan, doma-doma. (*Flicks Beggar's ear.*) Ordonyor!
When strong man tease you for laugh, you vex, but never
pick a fight. Lazyeeeeeeeeeeeeeee . . . (*Takes his skull-cap
off. Touches Beggar lightly on the face. Slaps his face hard. He
enjoys his own joke.*) Orgorrawdor! When women taunt
you left, right and centre, shaming you, you dance and
clown about. Okobo manja. Sonny Hoggy; You roll an'
roll from groun' to bed. (*He claps his hands in the air and
dances around.*) Kan-kan, doma-doma. Kan-kan, doma-
doma, Kan-kan doma-doma. Soon as kids come passin'
talkin', you run wild crazy. Stoning and cursing their
parents. Disecting the every size of their genitals. Kan-kan,
doma-doma, kan-kan, doma-doma, kan-kan, doma-doma.
(*He tickles his underfoot. Beggar kicks into the air.*) As for
me, am his greatest and most detested enemy. The unkind
friend who busy-body too much around. The unsym-
pathetic foolish brother . . . That's some of the scandalous
names he has since baptized me with . . . But he is me. I

am him. Inseparables. I am how he should be for real. The true blood of blood anyway. I am he that he resents. The light of his past; mirror of his present; torch for his future. I am his shadow in all and one, omnipotent. Omniscient, omnipresent.

BEGGAR (*grunts as he rolls over*): Blast, blast, blast. Go away. You are always interfering, nose-poking and spoiling my many good chances. Blast, blast, blast!

SHADOW: See what I mean? Blast, blast, blast like dynamite exploding. He blasts me a thousand and one times a day. He really dislike me. I am what I am, which he hates. He knows, that I know what I know, about him which is false and he sells. (*Pause.*) I hear what he thinks, which I know is not him. Kan-kan, doma-doma, kan-kan, doma-doma. (*He sits. Begins to root his hair again.*) You see, I tug at his ear lobes everytime he lies, brags and gets too conceited for those rags and tatters. He needs the pulling and shaking as often as possible to remind him of his present status, circumstances and conditions. If not he will be heading for psychiatric treatment or worse still the suicide gang. (*Very concerned.*) He is a misfit like them all. A real nuisance of a tramp. Rather seasoned parasite. An able scheming two-faced, tongue-twisting rogue. Never out of trouble. Double trouble finder. And for both of us . . . (*Despondently.*) God alone knows what he'll be up to when his tired eyelids part open and his senses relieved of the alcoholic stupor. Ha: liquor no good. You drink, the damn thing go down your stomach, next thing your head begin to dance like 'Sally-wan-sie'. This kin' of whiteman ju-ju sef, man nor fit understan'. How then we think say we understin' how the whiteman fit turn-turn an' twist-twist our big people like useless plate lying doing nothing. Whiteman lie-lie an' sweet-sweet ju-ju don' upset the worl' bad . . . Liquor ehn! For three days an' night we go from one wake to another. House to house, mourning. We walk in sorrowful and with sympathy. We stagger out drunk an' cursing. We are always chief mourners. Sometimes, he is relative and I am friend to the deceased. Come one, come all. No need for invitation to wakes. At least, it has not yet been discussed in Parliament yet. Besides, the new Parliamentarians themselves like going to wakes because they cannot yet afford to buy whisky out of their salary. When they have learnt how to take bribe, the subject of being selective and acquiring invitations to wakes will come up in Parliament as an important bill. Then we will find our courage and 'Unity' again and vote them out of power like we did their predecessors who came with all sorts of mad reforms and suggestions thinking we are a mad people without heads. Ha, well, they soon found out when they were out, that it is we who allow them to get fat and build up riches for themselves. But it is also we who destroy them. For had it not been our humanitarian understandings, not one of them could have had the chance of saving a million and more in Switzerland, London, America and all those other places. Oh yes, we know. We are not blind. We know. But, *'how for do?'* Where you tie a cow, that's where it should eat grass. Look at him. (*Points to Beggar.*) Can't blame him, can you? I mean what can a man do when he is a nowhere man. A nobody's friend . . . What do you expect of a self-confessed Misplaced man? What chances has a displaced tyrant? Have you ever heard of any unplaced prophet winning the hearts of his own people? Have you? What is he to do now when his total means of existence and livelihood depends wholly and solely on how excellent he's able to tell lies, talk big, brag, pull quick tricks and cut-in-big bluffs. (*Eyes Beggar despairingly.*) Hell, I wonder what he'll be having up his sleeves today since he's been sleepin' for so long. Hell, the damn truth is, even I being his shadow, guardian and all that, I cannot sometimes cope. He has a little mind full of conceit, impertinence, roguery. (*Gets up.*) Kan-kan, doma-doma, kan-kan, doma-doma, kan-kan, doma-doma. I too have to think. It is very necessary. Very, very necessary. As a shadow, I too have to lead sometimes, rather than just keep following. Depending on where the sun cast its blasted rays. How it shines, and what uncommunicated decision my good *here* friend makes. Most important is, which path of 'Wanderment' he decides to follow. (*Sighs.*) Mad though as he might seem, and materially deprived: he makes more sense than many of our categorized Honourables, Bookmen and those knowledgeable intellectual freaks. (*Spitefully, cynically.*) All decent pigs in white stainless garments and filthy hogs in attitude and behaviour towards their fellowmen. From pillar to post in our many untiring endless wanderments, there's been nothing but crucial contempt, disillusion, frustration and castigations. Not a day goes without such diabolic confrontations and humiliation . . . Oh these embarrassments! (*Hitting his head.*) Forget, forget, forget. Think not, remember none. Don't think, forget; don't think, forget; don't think. Kan-kan, doma-doma, kan-kan, doma-doma, kan-kan, doma-doma. Why the damn hell don't they invite people like us to weddings, christenings, hawujor and komorjada? Why? What is the world coming to, eh? What a dumpy-greedy-selfish bunch of un-neighbourly people. Why am I alive? Why are you living? (*Begins to beat the Beggar.*) Die, die, die, die, so I can vanish into oblivion. Die, die, die and leave this all-hateful people in their horrible world of deceit and power and murder. Die, die, and let us escape from this mean misery. Die, die. (*The beating and crying brings the Beggar to his senses. He hits Shadow hard across the face.*)

BEGGAR (*with violent madness*): You foolish man of barren stock, always turning your bottom to the mountain winds after you've drunk yourself to krais. Blast, blast, blast you. Damn you. How dare you come to a king's palace and take such liberty? Where are the guards? (*He calls*) Guards, guards. (*Like an authority giving orders.*) Take this *thing* away to the dungeon specially built for the likes of them. (*With calm.*) If there is anything I can't stand, insubordination is one of the many. Disrespect is another. And all that blast, blast, blast. This is exactly what our people mean, when they say, 'if you lie low at ease with underdogs in their fleas-wracked kernel, you are sure to rise half dead with poisoned bites'. I gave you an inch of man-to-man toleration and encouragement, now you have gone and taken advantage of my hospitality. Why is it got to be so difficult for kindness to be shown to you people of cowdung and dirt? Why can't you help yourself out of your misery and filth when merciful eyes lend you a glimpse of hope and faith? (*Sits and sighs.*) Well I can't sleep again.

SHADOW: So, what next?

BEGGAR: What do you mean, what next? I say, I can't sleep again and that is just because you fat whalemouth have been on your usual 'Sharowyaeing'. Blast, blast, blast. I wish the police would pick you up for nonsensical sabotage like, public masturbation.

SHADOW: I know the police does not really yet know their arse from their elbow. Still they will have to think twice before putting me in. Now what are the plans for today? Begging, bragging, cursing?

BEGGAR: Blast, blast, blast.

SHADOW: Lying, cheating, tricking.

BEGGAR: I wish I could magic you away from my sight and side. Blast, blast, blast!

SHADOW: Now stop your bla, bla, bla.

BEGGAR: Get away. Go; I want you to get lost. I have a long, long journey to battle with and I don't want you tailing me. Hear? I want to cross Obasai into Gbakanda-land. They are having their new year human sacrifice celebrations tonight.

SHADOW (*sings and claps*): Kan-kan, doma-doma, kan-kan,

doma-doma, kan-kan battle doma-doma, Journey doma-doma.

BEGGAR (*laughs to himself. Relaxes as if he has just discovered a new trick or secret*): Ha yes. Yesterday.

SHADOW (*eagerly*): What about yesterday?

BEGGAR: Blast, blast, blast. Can't you let my mouth open and close and my words fall full weight on the ground before you pick them up? Chai! You trick smell like King Jimmy closet.

SHADOW: Not more than the rags of him that I've all these difficult years followed, guard and direct.

BEGGAR: You wait. Just you wait. Soon, very soon, I will magic rid of you and that will be the end. The very end. I promise you. I will trade you to those Gbakanda savages. Tonight.

SHADOW: Until death do us part. Have you forgotten the bonds. Or is your old sickness of aberration back again? (*Pause.*) Kan-kan, doma-doma, Gbakanda doma-doma, Gbakanda-doma-doma.

BEGGAR (*rather exasperated*): Ka-ka, do-da-do-da. (*Shouts.*) Shut up. And I mean tight up you Gumption. Twerp! I am thinking of the Poda-poda fares from here to Gbakandaland.

SHADOW: Let's start on the journey now. (*He rises and dances off, singing.*) Kan-kan, doma-doma, kan-kan, doma-doma.

BEGGAR (*watches him go. Silently he looks up at the sky. Then in the direction where Shadow went off. Quietly and without anger*): Today is not my day. At least it does not seem so. Nature is against me. The sun directs my shadow to lead, which means that I must follow. But he doesn't know the way to Gbakandaland. What fate then has, lies ahead. (*Rather resigned.*) Tell me, how can a man be a man, a real full-blooded grown-up man, when he has to follow against his own wish? Blast, blast, blast. What a devil of a confusion it all is, eh? Jonah today, Daniel tomorrow. When not in a whale belly, I'm burnin' in a bush. Blast, blast, blast the whole thing stinks of blast, blast, blast.

Handsome with dimples one day, grey and twisted with
wrinkles another day. Now he has gone and left me here.
How do I know I am not going to starve with him playing
Herod and I looking up, Lazarus in ashes. Blast, blast,
blast, who'd ever want to exchange a palace for a goddamn
prison. (*Chuckles.*) Well, I suppose I am not the only one
in this state at the moment. There are Dictators, Kings,
Presidents and Prime Ministers all over the damn wretched
place exiled or imprisoned or both. God alone knows what
Tshombe, Kasavubu and Lumumba will be doing now in
the valley – yonder, from where no one comes to tell the
latest gossip. They were better off than me in them days.
Now I am a better man for what it's worth to be alive.
Blast, blast. I must go before he makes things chaotic
over there in Gbakandaland. Plenty of drinking and
feasting to be done, who knows I might even discover a
warm sleeping place: luxury they call it. Cool luxury in
Gbakandaland. Here in this damn Obasai we suffer from
chronic conservatism. No one cares about you when you
are alive, when you are dead they are happy to bury you
as if you were their burden. (*Looks around, he dashes off,
shouting.*) Blast, blast, blast! The hell. Kan-kan, doma-doma.
Where are you? Blast, blast you. Blast, blast, blast.

ACT ONE: SCENE TWO

*A faint lantern light reveals part of a forest. For a while, all is silent.
Gradually slow rhythm followed by movements of bodies in various
directions. Movements are as such, that they suggest a divine
reverence. As the light gets brighter, we see four strong masculine
bodies miming ritualistically grave-digging, or something which
looks as such, to the dirge which accompanies their movement. For
music see p. 158.*

GBAKS:
Sie-Nandae
ay-ay-ayaaaaaaaaaaaaa

Sie-Nandae-oooooooooo
Sie-Nandae
ay-ay-ayaaaaaaaaaaaaaa
Sie-Nandae-oooooooooooooooo
Tee-Gbengbeh ku-lorlee.

The dirge continues. It gets louder and louder. Lights increase revealing men in red-and-white striped sleeveless small shirts. They wear black-and-white striped baggy pants, hemmed with raffia at the end. Their ankles and wrists jingle with armulets. Each of them wears a mask and carries either a shovel, hoe, or pick-axe. As their singing gets louder, their movements increase in tempo and become more exaggerated.)

GBAKS:

Sie-Nandae
Ay-ay-ayaaaaaaaaaaaaaaa
Sie-Nandae-oooooooooooooo
Sie-Nandae
Ay-ay-ayaaaaaaaaaaaaaaaaa
Sie-Nandae-oooooooooo
Tee-Gbengbeh ku-lorlee . . .

1ST. GBAK *(comes forward demanding with a gesture, a wife)*: Min emba'kor.

2ND GBAK *(shaking his head in protest)*: 'Ur yaem'ong. Min emba'kor.

GBAKS:

Sie-Nandae
Ay-ay-ayaaaaaaaaaaaaaaaaaa
Sie-Nandae-oooooooooo
Sie-Nandae
Ay-ay-ayaaaaaaaaaaaa
Sie-Nandae-oooooooooooo
Tee-Gbengbeh ku-lorlee

3RD GBAK *(comes forward. Imploring for a wife he claims a right to have)*: Min em ba' kor. *(He does it to Second Gbak, all the others react disapproving.)*

2ND GBAK *(with much sterner refusal)*: 'Ur yaem 'ong. Yaem

'ong. Yaem 'ong. (*Fourth Gbak does the same. He too gets the same rebuff.*)

GBAKS:

No woman is ours. Not at this time
We need no wife. Not at this hour
We have no right to think of women
We have no time to feel for women
Not at this time
Not at this hour
Not in this place
To think of women
To think on women.

(*From a distance a woman's voice lamenting can be heard faintly. As if in distress.*)

UMU (*off-stage*):

Gbana oh. Gbana
Gbana come oh. Gbana come
Come and take me away with you. Come oh. Come
I am the unspoilt bride chosen for you
don't leave me to the scorn of Gbakandaland
I am Umu the girl you married at birth
Your parents chose me
My parents accepted
The gods' will
The Oracle decides
We accept their decisions.
Gbana oh, Gbana Bendu. My man, my master, my
    father.
Come oh. Come.

(*The Gbakandas continue their ritual in a listening pace. Dancing and humming.*)

UMU (*still off-stage, drawing nearer*):

Gbana oh. Gbana-Bendu
Where are you these many nights
When all the devils
of Gbakanda prong me hot with scorching spears.

New Year is near, Gbana is not here. Umu lives in fear
Gbana come oh, come to my rescue.

1ST GBAK: The Oracle keeps drawing her nearer and nearer.

4TH GBAK: Soon, very soon, the bitch will be exorcized from
our midst.

UMU: They will not let me know peace by day nor rest by
night. Why?

3RD GBAK: Because you nar 'Kriffi sarra Umu. You are the
sacrifice for Gbakanda's New Year . . . Ur' Tamrokoh
prayed. The gods will the Oracle decide, Gbana Bendu
the Invisible must have you.

GBAKS:

She knows her duty. Grant her that. The gods' laws know
no appeal. The Oracle's decision stands supreme and final.
We too, Umu like you, some day have got to go. Where
we go; to perish, suffer or gain, we know not. Go we must,
go we must.

(*They break into a strong hunting dirge and dancing. For music
see p. 158.*)

Go we must go daan d'wu meh.

Go you must go daan d'wu meh

Umu da go daan d'wu meh

Nar go you for go

Danna d'wu meh, dan d'wu meh, daan d'wu meh.

(*They repeat the song, dancing and leaping into the air.
Gradually a great flat stone which has all this time been hidden
is revealed. They dance round the stone which is approximately
centre stage. It is around this stone that they have been doing the
previous movements.*)

2ND GBAK: Gbakandas will go; Gbakandas must go.

GBAKS: New Year takes beautiful Gbakanda daughters
New Year kills strong Gbakandas who know no fear.

2ND GBAK

Ur' Tamrokoh prays
The gods will
The Oracle decides

D

GBAKS:

    Whatever the lot and on whose head it falls

    It is New Year's Sacrifice for great and for small.

UMU (*off-stage*):

    Lead me oh thou great Jehovah

    to the place where I can find my lover

    take me to my heart's desire

    him to whom my parents gave me

    him for whom alone I live

    take me, take me to my master's presence

    life is dead without him by me

    love is not with us two parted

    take oh take the servant to the master

    I am lost my heart is breaking.

4TH GBAK: She's a good choice for the Oracle. What a damn shame ...

3RD GBAK: We cannot let her come here and desecrate our ancient respected secret society. Besides, she's going to upset the task Ur' Tamrokoh has set us to do.

2ND GBAK: The Sarra of the gods, the Oracle of the New Year must be fulfilled and realized by desecration in defilement ...

1ST GBAK: You are young. You know not the procedures of the shrewd and wily Ur' Tamrokoh.

3RD GBAK: But, but, but we just can't. It will mean our destruction as well. Ur' Tamrokoh warned us against defilement and uncircumcised intruders.

2ND GBAK: We are the Gbakandas. The seed and roots of all destructions. The undestroyed.

GBAKS:

    We are the Gbakandas, first and last.

    Sons of great Gbakandas, killers of men.

    We live Gbakandas, fearless;

    We die Gbakandas undefeated.

    We travel supreme. Gbakandas now, Gbakandas forever.

2ND GBAK:

    The depth of all Seven seas.

GBAKS:

Contain not the immortal secrets of the ancient rites and ancestral rituals of Gbakanda land.

2ND GBAK:

The vastness of the blanketed changing clouds, from earth's beginning to the world's eternity.

GBAKS:

Can't boast of as much knowledge and plentiful wisdom as we Gbakandas.

2ND GBAK:

The daring glare; the desert's heir, hot scorching sun.

GBAKS:

Brow beat no bead off Gbakanda sweat from Gbakandas' face.

2ND GBAK:

Strike swords on Akpata rock.

GBAKS:

Gbakandas' stroke rent clouds asunder . . . Split skies apart.

2ND GBAK:

Splash, lightning splash.

GBAKS:

Gbakandas laugh.

2ND GBAK:

Cloudbelly complain hungry.

GBAKS:

Gbakandas frown.

2ND GBAK:

Red sun and full moon intersect.

Gbakanda is born. Gbakanda strong.

UMU (*enters quietly talking to herself*): It is dark. I grope my way like Oku the Blind who knows neither day nor night. Blunder in wanderments like Jaynet Bundle. Hither and thither, searching, hunting and hoping. Hoping.

2ND GBAK: Beware Umu. Beware you uninitiated sacrifice to the gods. The gods' trap of Gbakanda does not relent neither does it release . . .

GBAKS: Beware Umu the paths on which you have chosen to walk. Beware woman of infamy, beware daughter of ignommy. (*She walks towards them slowly and directly. Third Gbak produces a rope which he offers to the others for tying up Umu. They all refuse to accept or confront her. He folds the rope and with all his mustered anger throws it at Umu. She stops and stares at them.*)

1ST GBAK: Strike koboko on hot brown earth.

GBAKS: Foolish rage from scare and bark with fear.

UMU (*sternly*): Ungodly men go mad and impotent.

GBAKS: Softly, softly foolish barren maid.

2ND GBAK: There will be no going back.

3RD GBAK: No back-talk, Umu. No back-talk.

4TH GBAK: Blessed and free are those that love in spirit.

GBAKS: For the flesh in love moralizes in sticky stains, wallowing in disrepute.

2ND GBAK: Let birds in love be steadfast.

GBAKS: While men professing love learn diligence.

UMU: It is Gbana I seek.

GBAKS: He is not here and that you know full well.

1ST GBAK: You have no right to come looking for him.

UMU: I have all right to seek him anywhere.

GBAKS: Umu, daughter from a pithless spine, you talk too fast.

UMU: Don't you know why?

4TH GBAK: You have been warned child of congealed sperm.

2ND GBAK: Alaki pekin watin make you tranga yase so?

GBAKS:

We bin don' warn you oh Umu

teda, tumarra, leh den nor go say nar we put you pan nambarra.

Nar you sef take you han' kam fen plaba

We nor bin da when Joki banda bin da burn . . .

Gbana whey nar 'im you lek

we sef lek am

Gbana whey nar im you da look for

Nar 'im we da wok for now, now
Gbana whey you nor know
Nar we yone big Bra
Gbana whey you marrade to
Nar we yone master
But you bin for ask fus
watin 'E Be
You bin for take tem ask good
Who dat 'E be.

UMU: But it is not our customs, you know it. Questions are unasked. Arguments unheard of when the gods will and the Oracle decides. I am married to Gbana. To Gbana am married.

GBAKS: New Years' wedding, sacrificial blessing.

UMU: The gods will, the Oracle decides.

2ND GBAK (*fiercely*): Like all brides of New Year, you have defiled our most sacred ground. Like all brides of Gbana-Bendu, you have defied our ancient laws and customs. Like all Gbakandas' uninitiated and accursed you have desecrated the holy shrine of Gbana-Bendu. You have penetrated the forbidden of the gods.

UMU: And so I am to suffer?

GBAKS: Yes. Yes. Yes. Yes.

UMU: I stand ready. Here, do with me what you may.

GBAKS: We warned you Umu. You ignored us.

2ND GBAK: Faal whey nor yeri Sheeeee ... Go ... Go ... yeri stone.

(*They gather round* UMU *and begin to chant. She tries to move out, but every way she turns she is stopped by one of the Gbakandas. Their movements are strong and suggestive of violence.*)

GBAKS:
Sie-Nandae
Ay-ay-ayaaaaaaaaaaaaaaaaaaaaaaaaaaaaaaaaaa
Sie-Nandae ohooooo
Sie-Nandae
Ay-ay-ayaaaaaaaaaaaaaaaaaaaaaaaaaa

Sie-Nandae ohooooo
Te-Gbengbah ku-lorlee
Te-Gbengbeh ku-lorlee.

(UMU *stands in the midst of them as they dance round her. She is about 18 years. Dressed in white long wrapper. She is bare-footed and without head dress. She is tall and brown in complexion. Her expression is sorrowful, though she has a strong personality. The Gbakandas continue their dancing as if ready for the kill.*)

2ND GBAK (*grabbing Umu from the back*): What say you woman of straws?

1ST GBAK: Chop off her stubborn head.

3RD GBAK: Slice off her stone breast. (*They close in on her. She is forced to sit uneasily cowering.*)

2ND GBAK: Not yet, not yet. Umu has got something to tell us. (*He holds on to her mouth as if choking her. She struggles but in vain.*) That something which brought you here. That urge that made you defy the gods, challenge the Oracle and disrespect Ur' Tamrokoh our immortal father. (*They put her to lie on the Akpata rock.*)

1ST GBAK: Sit you sef down and speak.

3RD GBAK (*shouts*): Speak before I flash my matchet (*picks up a matchet by the edge of the stone*) and trample your headless uninitiated body into dry cowdung. Speak! I'll make her talk good and proper. (*He pulls her ear.*)

GBAKS: Talk Mumu, talk. Talk Umu, talk. Do you know Gbana? Have you seen Gbana? Who told you to come here at this time of year and night? Talk Umu, talk. Speak Mumu, speak.

3RD GBAK (*pulls her hair*): Talk. Talk. Talk Mumu, talk.

GBAKS: You taunt Gbana; you hunt Gbana.

3RD GBAK: You make trouble for you; you make trouble for us.

2ND GBAK: Know you not who Gbana was?

UMU: Until we meet face to face, you tell me now who Gbana is.

GBAKS: Gbana-Bendu, no woman eyes behold. Gbana-

Bendu, no woman will ever meet. Gbana-Bendu of Gbakanda destroys the woman kind, like Umu's type. All woman kind. Umu's type.

UMU: You tongue-twisting deceiters. You blemish satans of Gbakandaland.

2ND GBAK: Oh madness, it knows no shame. You are gone, Umu. Far gone to the dogs.

GBAKS: Ah, the gods will, the Oracle decides. Umu must perish. Her beauty is cancerous, rebellious, obscene.

3RD GBAK: Detribalized shrew.

UMU: Your traditions deprive me of my rights.

2ND GBAK: Only the powerful speak of rights.

UMU: Antiquated customs rob me of my womanhood.

GBAKS: If you speak of Gbana, he is neither Yours nor Ours. Never has been, never will be possessed by One in love, he loves.

2ND GBAK: Love is not in Gbana's hut. Love is void in Gbana's loins.

UMU: He possessed me. I am his wife, his New Year's bride. His own, his very soul.

GBAKS: The gods will Umu to madness. The Oracle decides your beauty treacherous. Traditions gave you up from birth to perish. Ur' Tamrokoh possessed your mind to destroy your body.

2ND GBAK: You, Umu, like a chick hatched like akuru dog will die. For vultures to devour. Gone fape and forgotten. Possessing, possessed, possession, klap han', klap foot. Nothing brought, nothing to carry.

UMU (*shouts*): Gbana ohoo. Gbana deliver me from these cannibal monsters.

3RD GBAK: When has it become the custom for a wife to go hunting her husband in Gbakandaland?

UMU: I am a wife that knows her rights.

4TH GBAK (*laughing*): We people always say 'teeth knows no mourning'.

2ND GBAK: She talks too fast.

1 ST GBAK: Her tongue is sharp.

UMU: Because you unclean sons of Gbakanda do me wrong . . . so speak I must. I will . . .

3RD GBAK (*sarcastically*): Until your life light is restored ehn?

UMU: Till my womanhood is fulfilled.

3RD GBAK: By way of demonstrating feminine emancipated disrespect, ehn?

UMU (*as if mad, she demands*): Where is Gbana-Bendu? Who among you killed him? (*With spiteful venom.*) You sons of Krifi, murderers. (*She spits.*)

2ND GBAK: What do you talk, Umu?

GBAK: Of Krifi? Of murder?

2ND GBAK: Why, you daughter of Krifi, born and bought and sold . . .

GBAKS: Child of the twin-tongue viper. Woman with a heart of stone . . .

1 ST GBAK: Wombless spike-bush of an abdomen.

GBAKS: Don't you understand? Don't you know, we know who trick-choked the father of Gbana-Bendu.

4TH GBAK: Did we not uncover who cooked the concocted Attefoh' palava sauce.

GBAKS: Most poisonous 'Medicine for love'.

1 ST GBAK: Prepared and seasoned in Borfima's fat . . .

4TH GBAK: Spiced with iguana intestines. Cooked in egusi of dry pounded cockroaches.

2ND GBAK: Sprinkled hot parched Fangay for redpepper.

3RD GBAK (*shouts*): Water, give me . . . Gbana shouted.

GBAKS (*despairingly*): Water . . . when it came . . . Oh you unsleeping gods, never forgive them. Water, scented water, Lasmamy water . . .

UMU (*raising her hand above her head protesting*): Not guilty. Not guilty. You lie, lie, lie, most pernicious, all treacherous lies invented.

GBAKS:

The gods will your disgraceful doom.

The Oracle decided a pitiless fate.

UMU:

Nearer my God I know
Faraway from your gods of woe.

2ND GBAK: Daughter of ill devices, child of sterility, your kind have long plagued our tribe.

1ST GBAK: New Year is here, your price is fair.

GBAKS: The self-same price your mother's mother's mother paid for their foolish schemings.

3RD GBAK: Life is dear, life is sweet but not for Umu.

GBAKS: See how she glitters, child of mould.

4TH GBAK: You did put out your own candle.

GBAKS:

When you die, as you die,
the grave's not your end
death's trap is not the goal.

UMU: Must I die because I love?

GBAKS: Like your mother's mother's mother.

2ND GBAK: Oh the deceitful hyena; see how she glows in the glory of her Chameleon changelings.

GBAKS: Like her mother's mother's mother. Same soup in different dish.

3RD GBAK: What next, brown beauty?

4TH GBAK: Alas, black-ebony beast.

1ST GBAK: How fare you in this your hour of transitional change?

2ND GBAK: From life lived to deaths' experience, ehn?

UMU (*holding her head high. With calm*): Proud enough to realize the transition which is yet to assure you of power and make you feel certain of your triumph. I do promise you though, that my dead body in your bloody hands will grace with shame your murderous traditions. Sacrifice I am. Yes, a human sacrifice.

2ND GBAK: You speak too hot.

1ST GBAK: Your tongue is sharp.

UMU (*coolly*): You must purify your secret society bush by

violently sacrificing Umu. Your crops will not grow, your wives will not give birth, your gods will not be gods, your Oracle will not bless you unless you slaughter a human being like you do cows, and goats and pigs for your many horror sacrifices. My blood must be your communion wine and my meat your most delicate supper. New Year's feast. Come on blood brothers of Gbakanda. Come rip into pieces Umu the fearless maid of Gbakanda. Daughter of Po-Joe, bride to Gbana-Bendu. Come. Let your cruel hands of futility dismember my body of Gbakanda. Wrench out my heart of love. Come, come and silence my spirit of generous courage, kill my will, freeze my rights. Come, come take my life; take it, it is all. It is all I have and what you need most. (*Begins to sing, rather wild and desperately.*)

Take my life and make it thine
consecrate it for your shrine
help your gods to reach my God
leave the devil, God will bless you.

3RD GBAK: Shut up, you wicked witch. Shut up.

UMU (*leaps to her full height. They move a little away from her*): You dreamers. You who know that I know what you know.

GBAKS: What?

UMU: You want money?

GBAKS: Don't you?

UMU: You want fame?

GBAKS: Don't you?

1ST GBAK: If not why go in desperate search for Gbana the rich, the powerful and unidentified?

UMU: You enjoy your life of destructive gaiety.

GBAKS: Don't envy us.

UMU: You make the forest your possession. The grave your shrine. Dig up the dead and steal from the dead and sell to the fools. Now you want to kill not to be exposed.

1ST GBAK: How would you like a villa on the Riviera?

2ND GBAK: A Mercedes Benz automatic, chauffeur driven?

4TH GBAK: City flat, servants and maids, waiting with trays of gold. Champagne on ice for breakfast with leg of chicken.

3RD GBAK: Wine and lobster for lunch.

2ND GBAK: Make your choice for supper. Forget who pays. Order, order, order.

1ST GBAK: It is all there for the asking. Eat, drink and be merry.

4TH GBAK: Ask no questions and you'll win a billion dollar bill.

UMU: You disgust me, Gbakandas of innumerable characters. Dregs, thieves. Acquaintances of murderous delights.

1ST GBAK: Oh, puny woman. Acquaintances have short coming effects, friends long lasting defects and unaccountable disparity. Dig?

UMU: You seek contentment?

2ND GBAK: Nothing sought after, nothing gained.

4TH GBAK: Contentment soothes individuals.

1ST GBAK: Whether in exile, at home, wherever and whenever, whatever, happens, let it contain contentment.

3RD GBAK: High or low, sea or sky.

2ND GBAK: Contentment is me. Undivided individual.

UMU: Much worse than the worst, you've said of yourselves.

1ST GBAK: The benefits of obscurity are innumerable and incalculable.

UMU: My ignominy, I won't share with the infamous, corrupt Gbakandas.

2ND GBAK: We are distinguished with distinction.

UMU: It takes all sorts to make the human kind in this insecure world of mixed races and creeds.

1ST GBAK: Realize this. You must die here Umu.

UMU: I have heard too much of your treachery, deceit and guilt, you brothers of Gbakanda. (*Picking up one of the matchets lying by the edge of the akpata stone.*) You sons of Gbakanda. (*Brandishing the matchet in front of their faces.*) You creeping cursed reptiles (*She invites them to an open fight.*) I challenge you to prove your might. Pit your strength the four of you and Umu will match you one by one. (*Beating her breast.*) Come, kill me now. Take me live if you dare to face your elders. I challenge you. Fight, fight, if not I will go on to defile your very gods and shrine and Oracle and secret society and New Year. Come on fight, fight. (*They are all holding matchets. Walking round the akpata stone for the rest of the dialogues.*)

4TH GBAK: Oh madness that knows no shame.

2ND GBAK: You are mad, mad, mad, mad.

UMU: Like all sacrifices of the New Year.

3RD GBAK: You talk too swift, you know it stinks.

1ST GBAK: Your tongue is sharp.

2ND GBAK: Umu daughter, inheritor of poisonous foods, for many you and your mother's mother's mother have cooked . . .

UMU: Lies. Look at your disfigured faces in the murderous mirrors of each other's eyes. Look and see your naked souls of foul play.

2ND GBAK: Now many will cook and watch you eat.

1ST GBAK: To perish, Umu. To perish and die.

UMU: For your mercies and forgiveness, let me perish.

GBAKS: The gods will, the Oracle decides.

UMU: Sons of nogood. Children of injustice. Friends of evils and comrades of death. Light your owlfire. Rejoice and cook your Awujoh food. Mundoh your outrageous lusts with greed and hate. Stir your Fangay cauldrons. Pass round the gourds of Borfima soup. (*She bursts out laughing. It becomes hysterical and uncontrollable. The four Gbakandas assume a position of both defence and attack. Umu gets more hysterical until she finally breaks out into a ritual song and dance with a desperate frenzy. Like a mad killer.*)

You beat me teda

Nar da Gbakanda

So fight-fight

So fight Gbakanda

(*As Umu sings the Gbakanda sing back the refrain at the same time circling the stone and hitting it with their matchet.*)

GBAKS:

Gbone-gbone
Gbone-Gbana oh
so fight, fight, so fight Umu oh
You beat me teda
nar da Gbana oh
so fet-fet
So fet Umu oh.

(*They fence. Umu and First Gbakanda. The others watch very concerned as they sing.*)

GBAKS:

Gbone-gbone
Gbone-Gbana Oh
so fight-fet and die Umu oh.

(*The First Gbakanda gets tired; he falls out and is relieved by Second Gbak.*)

2ND GBAK:

Aggo kill you teda
Nor body go know.

GBAKS:

So fet, fet
so fet Umu oh
Gbone, gbone-Gbana oh
so fet, fet
So fet Umu ohooo.

(*The fight continues and the others go on singing.*)

4TH GBAK: Fight. Fight you uncircumcised provoker of the dead. Fight and be equalled to the condemned.

(*The dance gets wilder and more uncontrollable. Seemingly from nowhere emerge creatures human from the waist down, but from the torso and heads upwards of animals or birds or reptiles. They join the singing and improvise dancing according to their species. For music see p. 158. Occasionally they come out with eerie sounds. The fighting gets wilder. The atmosphere becomes confused and frenzied. Third Gbak relieves Second. Umu dances wildly and groggily.)*

UMU (*wild and fierce*):
You kill me teda
Nar da Gbana oh.

GBAKS:
So fight-fet
and kill teda oh
Gbone-gbone Gbana oh
So fight-fet
and kill teda oh.

UMU:
You beat me teda.

GBAKS:
Nar da Gbana oh.

UMU:
You kill oh
you kill Gbana oh.

GBAKS:
Gbone, gbone Gbana oh.

UMU:
I know oh
You kill Gbana oh.

GBAKS:
Gbone, gbone Gbana oh
We nor know oh
Who kill Gbana oh
Gbone, gbone Gbana oh.

(Fourth Gbak relieves Third. They all close in on her with excessive wildness.)

GBAKS:
We go kill you teda
nar you sef fen am
zo-wa-wa
zo-wa-Umu oh

Gbone, gbone Gbana oh
Zo-wa-wa

(*They press in on her. The noises of the creatures blare all over the place. Umu gives a long scream. A complete silence.*)

UMU (*breathless*): Kill me like you killed Gbana-Bendu. Kill me. Kill.

Enter Ur'Tamrokoh in a knee-length sheepskin gown and woollen cap of bright colours pulled down to his ears. He is of medium height and heavily built. He wears hand-made skin slippers and carries a staff neatly wound with animal skins. His presence is immediately felt. He gives his sneeze – a symbol of his authority. See p. 159.

UR'TAMROKOH:

T'nseecnh oh T'nseecnh krappo T'nseecnh oh
T'nseecnh oh T'nseecnh krappo T'nseecnh oh.

The creatures fall flat on their faces. Umu remains lying flat on the Akpata stone. The Gbakandas go down on their knees.

GBAKS:

Ur'Tamrokoh Yan-ka-di Ba-ba
Ur'Tamrokoh Yan-ka-di Ba-ba.

UR'TAMROKOH:

T'nseecnh oh T'nseecnh oh
Krappo T'nseecnh oh

You sons of Gbakanda, I send you here to execute a ritual. Not to persecute and destroy the sacrifice of that ritual.

2ND GBAK: She came among us, defiant of all our warnings.

UR'TAMROKOH: The gods will, the Oracle decides. (*With irony.*) Why avenge your anger on sterility, you who can kill elephants with matchets; paralyse lions with a hiss. Why invoke the wrath of our deads at such an hour o night when all is not humanly peaceful. (*As conjuring.*) Oh you spirits of the dead and dark, shadow them light as they go. (*He orders them.*) Get lost into the pestilence of darkness; and beware those sorefooted unsleeping night watchers with their flea-wracked mongrels.

1ST GBAK: We go to our sacred duties Ur'Tamrokoh.

4TH GBAK: Men and dogs can watch and bark. They have no might to presage Gbakandas might.

UR'TAMROKOH: Yan-ka-di.

2ND GBAK: We will not waste strength on flies by slapping broom on walls when hungry spiders share our hut.

UR'TAMROKOH: Even the fatigued strength of a Gbakanda we know will kill leopards, tame lions and uproot poisoned cotton trees.

1ST GBAK: Ur'Tamrokoh, father of Gbakandas. You who know our father's, father's, father's might.

2ND GBAK: Brave undying mediator of our gods.

3RD GBAK: Interpreter of men and beasts and birds and trees.

GBAKS: Despatch us with the tongues of the gods. Set us off with the action of the Oracle.

4TH GBAK: It is quiet and serene. Now is the time for us to plunder.

UR'TAMROKOH: The spider must hunt well when noising flies go berserk.

T'nseecnh oh. T'nseecnh oh
Kroppo T'nseecnh oh

GBAKS:

Ur'Tamrokoh father of rainbows.
Child of the sun and moon
spirit of the first fruits of Gbakanda
we dorballeh oh, as we go,
We dorballeh as we go into the night of nights.

UR'TAMROKOH:

The sacrifice must wander. Therefore avoid crossroads.
The gods will the 'Best' of goods.
The Oracle decides 'Stores of Bounty'.
T'nseecnh oh T'nseecnh oh
Krappo T'nseecnh oh.

1ST GBAK (*warning the others*):
No blunder as we plunder.

New Year comes with thunder.
Ur'Tamrokoh expect wonders.

UR'TAMROKOH:
The gods will, I don't.
The Oracle decides, I obey.

2ND GBAK: If not for trespassing, we would have long gone.

4TH GBAK (*pointing at Umu*): She challenged the might of the
Gbakandas. She . . .

UR'TAMROKOH:
T'nseecnh oh T'nseecnh
Krappo T'nseecnh oh
The sacrifice must wander into banishment. Madness
knows no stopping, plundering no mercy.
T'nseecnh oh T'nseecnh oh
Krappo T'nseecnh oh.
Oh yes, the bull is slain, the lion faint; the panther trapped,
mountains levelled. Hah, ha, ha. All is well, Ur'Tamrokoh
lives on to unravel the marvels of our gods and Oracles. To
interpret the dreams of the elders and the wishes of the
dead.

1ST GBAK: Pantheon of our land. Father of our father's,
father's, father. Defender of great and small in Gbakandaland. The night air welcomes us with coolness, the silence
promises New Year's bounty in great abundance. Bless
us as we go.

UR'TAMROKOH (*angry*): You noising hyenas, go. You
have too long provoked the spirit of the gods. You disturb the flowing peace of our deads by wasting time. You
know full well that daylight is an envious enemy of our
cult.

GBAKS: By the gods will, we go. With the Oracle's decision,
you predict our fate.

UR'TAMROKOH: Return well loaded, bountifully with plenty,
for the harvest must provide for all and left overs for dogs.

GBAKS:
Yan-ka-di Ba-ba

peace is here
New Year's peace.

UR'TAMROKOH:

The gods will, not I.
The Oracle decides, I obey.

GBAKS: Oh womb that bore us into this world. Oh mothers
of our mother's mother, remember us in your prayers to
the dead. Pour libations for us in your early hours of
rising.

UR'TAMROKOH:

T'nseecnh oh T'nseecnh oh
krappo T'nseecnh oh
T'nseecnh oh T'nseecnh oh
krappo T'nseecnh oh.

Leave no stains of black blood behind you. Avoid all
windy smells of scented impurity. Look you well and
careful for mixed signs of tomorrow's disgrace.

2ND GBAK:

Our mistakes will be our mothers' horrible fate.
Our disgrace will not make our brothers of Gbakanda
a better tomorrow in a happier state.

UR'TAMROKOH:

The gods will, I do not
The Oracle decides, I obey.

GBAKS: As the gods convene we go. On the Oracle's decision
we abide. Yan-ka-di. Ba-ba. Yan-ka-di. (*They back away.*)

UR'TAMROKOH (*waving them off*):

T'nseecnh oh T'nseecnh oh
krappo T'nseecnh oh
T'nseecnh oh T'nseecnh oh
krappo T'nseecnh oh . . .

For us there will be a happy and good New Year. Not so for
many. It is better to lose what you have in wealth than
to lose what you have in health. Go boys and bring me
wealth. Those who will not give willingly, must loose
unwillingly. We must kindle for them their own beliefs

and traditions. We must guide them as they have always been guided. To deprive them of their New Year's sacrifice would be considered a sacrilege, sabotage and anarchy. So it is only fair to uphold tradition even though it brings with it untold misery.

(*As the Gbakandas go away they chant the dirge of the Shrine: Sie-Nandae. Ur'Tamrokoh goes up to Umu.*)

GBAKS (*in the distance*):
Sie-Nandae
Ay-ay-ayaaaaa
Sie-Nandae ohhhhh
Sie-Nandae
Ay-ay-ayaaaaaa
Sie-Nandae ohhhhh
Tee-Gbengbeh ku-lorlee
Tee-Gbengbeh ku-lorlee

UR'TAMROKOH: Oh virgin with cowry eyes. My most dangerous New Year sacrifice. It was a good thing I came before they had their octopus fingers all over your jelly cream body. (*Lecherously.*) Ha, the gods know what to will and the Oracle what to decide upon.

UMU (*half rising. Dreamlike*): My mind, my eyes, my head . . . Have they gone?

UR'TAMROKOH: To return laden with New Year's wealth.

UMU: I am tired. I wish I did not allow myself to be bought so cheaply into such ghastly complications.

UR'TAMROKOH: The gods will, not you Umu. The Oracle decides. Tck, tck, tck, we obey, ehn?

UMU: In the meantime, what's happening?

UR'TAMROKOH: We will not be together. Not yet. You must go on your prescribed wanderings. (*Menacingly.*) There, as you wander you will find Him when the sun and the moon embrace in their final intercourse. When the old sprinkles sweet soft dew into the young, hot and reverberating. When New Year emerges strong and green with the old waxing strong and big inside the fragile hot young.

Then Umu, all will be rejoicing. The Oracle will have languished, the gods appeased and the sacrifice dispoiled. You would have been the happiest of brides in Gbakanda-land, most handsomely paid . . .

UMU: In the meantime my fate is madness.

UR'TAMROKOH: Have you heard of men violating the laws of society?

UMU: Yes!

UR'TAMROKOH: Rebel ehn? Have you ever heard of men going into the Bondo bush of vestal virgins? Even I, I Ur'Tamrokoh, I dare not confront those powers above and beyond that are not revealed to me through the gods. I seek not for the unknown secrets that are hidden away by those who best know how to guard them. I penetrate into that which I have full rights and power.

UMU: My trespasses are the gods' will and Ur'Tamrokoh's wish.

UR'TAMROKOH: The oracles approve, but sweet juicy angel of New Year, don't let your madness draw you near too early. Don't let childishness drunken you to confuse sacrilege with communion (*affectionately*) of evil conceit; oh scornful peril that we call Love . . . Umu, as you are now, I can see, your triumph of the New Year neither lips nor tongue of man can stop to tell its tale. You have done well. You have triumphed gloriously more than any maiden of Gbakanda.

UMU: Do I see in Ur'Tamrokoh my Gbana-Bendu?

UR'TAMROKOH: Oh, lascivious thoughts (*tries to control himself*) let us not bow so low in this open unguarded forest to our mutual emotions. The hour commeth when we sip the wine together, scratch our eyes out, spill blood of passion and eat compassionate food of potent Gbakanda poison. Let's be patient. It will all be soon over and we have a whole year of lascivious masquerades. (*The Gbakanda dirge begins to swell from a distance. The birds, animals and reptiles join in the singing.*) Go now and believe in what you

have been told to believe in. Go; do that which is traditional and which our ancestors inherited. We cannot change.
We are a constant people. You must not desert the course
you are to take. It is a thing unheard of in Gbakandaland.
Go, Umu, hurry before these canker worms raise their
voices in demand of your seasoned flesh. Go this way;
and listen, the quiet sleeper must have love dreams or
jump in his nightmares while the sons of Gbakanda make
their visitations. The sleepless must be frightened not to
arouse curiosity. Go, Umu, you know the way and play
the game too well.

UMU: I obey Master.

UR'TAMROKOH (*in feigning horror*): The adder is on your
trail. Your father preaches like Peter – 'He knows you not'.
The townsfolk await you with sharpened words that'd
pierce the ears of any bat.

UMU: The night is dark and young, but the task is hard and
difficult for a woman.

UR'TAMROKOH: You are in one, the beginning of the end.
The end of the circle. No other woman can succeed where
you fail . . . and you must succeed.

UMU: You are wicked; and only the strong can be as wicked
and cruel as you.

UR'TAMROKOH: It is a crime to be weak in this world where
only the all powerful rule and the all poor and weak
suffers.

UMU: Had I power enough, I would demand that justice
which would flow and follow Ur'Tamrokoh, his gods and
Oracle and those merciless plundering Gbakandas.

UR'TAMROKOH: The townsfolk will have you exorcised.
Never tamper with the faith of traditional folks. Myth is
in itself the lifeblood of many a race of people. Take away
their myth, you'll be hung, drawn and quartered; heresy,
anarchy, sorcery will be your charges, deserving crucifix-
ion. Martyrdom is not as glorified as it used to be. And
besides, go seek your father, he will tell you my stories.

Call all Gbakandas of repute and renown, they'll recount
my histories.

UMU: Tell me, Ur'Tamrokoh, Gbana-Bendu are you my
love?

UR'TAMROKOH: Love is our undoing. True life lived to-
gether knows no reasoning for such weaknesses.
L for Look; O for Observe; V for Venture; E for Escape.
Tchai . . . Love – what a blasphemy . . . passst.

UMU: My love makes me weaker. My Gbana-Bendu.

UR'TAMROKOH: If you have ears, you will go now. But
I advise you. Stop not on your way; neither look
back; nor ask for help or protection or love. Your world
and life are one vast stretch of winding footpath. You
have to pick your way out carefully. Alone. Until we
meet.

UMU: Never to part company?

UR'TAMROKOH: The gods will; the Oracle decides.

UMU: I am thirsty.

UR'TAMROKOH: The sky cannot cry now; neither can the
desert sand show pity. Go and stop fooling.

UMU: I will die, should they discover our game.

UR'TAMROKOH: A good consolation for the weak who
avoids naming names.

UMU: I never drank my bridal wine nor touched my bride-
groom's hand.

UR'TAMROKOH: In time, as the god's will; it will last when
the Oracle decides. Go now, I smell the unclean . . .
strangers are like bats. They go about with flapping ears.
And night has no secret since it has no eyes.

UMU: Bride sacrifice . . . New Year's gift . . .

UR'TAMROKOH: Had always happened. A blessing in dis-
guise.

UMU: It is dark. My eyes are heavy with sleeping scales.
Blow, blow harmattan winds. Blow me hard, blow me dry,
parch me all over, blow, blow burn me off.
(*As she walks away, the dirge which has been going on quietly*

gradually begins to swell up in tempo. The humanlike beasts
watch her go and so arrange themselves about Ur'Tamrokoh.)

BEASTS:
Sie-Nandae
Ay-ay-ayaaaaaaaaaaaa
Sie-Nandae
Sie Nandae
ay-ay-ayaaaaaaaaaaaa
Sie-Nandae ohoooooooo
Tee-Gbengbeh ku-lorlee
Tee-Gbengbeh ku-lorlee

UR'TAMROKOH (*on the Akpata stone*): Don't come near . . .
keep away dear, this place is sacred this ground is hot . . .

BEASTS:
Hot-hot red pepper; Gbakanda pepper
this bush is warm; Ur'Tamrokoh's blood is hot.

BEASTS:
Ur'Tamrokoh's tongue
all Gbakanda fear
Ur'Tamrokoh's bride
New Year's sacrifice
We know, we know, we know.

UR'TAMROKOH (*sleepily*): The gods will; I don't. The
Oracle decides; I obey . . .
(*A quick fade.*)

ACT ONE: SCENE THREE

It is nearly daybreak. The scene is set as in scene two. The beasts
have all disappeared. Ur'Tamrokoh is jubilantly dancing and
singing alone. The Beggar and Shadow are crouched together
secretly in a corner. They are worn out, haggard looking, hungry
and tired. They have been listening and watching Ur'Tamrokoh
who has not seen them, but has a feeling that he is being watched.

UR'TAMROKOH (*dances little steps, front, sideways and back*):
'A salaam ma laikun – it is good morning.

BEGGAR, SHADOW: Ma laikun wa salaam.

UR'TAMROKOH: 'A salaam ma laikun – me say good mornin'.

BEGGAR, SHADOW: Ma laikun – good mornin'.

UR'TAMROKOH: Dem nor know say teda, nar da;

BEGGAR, SHADOW: Zoh-wa-wa . . . zo wa.

UR'TAMROKOH: Dem nor know sef watin da be

BEGGAR, SHADOW: Never. Zoh wa-wa-zoh wa.

UR'TAMROKOH: Dem nor care why 'E da be.

BEGGAR, SHADOW: What for . . . Zoh-wa-wa . . . zoh wa.

UR'TAMROKOH: Den nor worry how 'E go be.

BEGGAR, SHADOW: Too bad. Zoh-wa-wa . . . Zoh wa . . .

UR'TAMROKOH: 'A salaam ma laikun – welcome New Year.

BEGGAR, SHADOW: Ma laikun sacrifice.

UR'TAMROKOH: 'A salaam ma laikun – what a happy morn.

BEGGAR, SHADOW: Ma laikun, New Year.

UR'TAMROKOH: I must go visit the town.

BEGGAR, SHADOW: Zoh-wa-wa; Zoh-wa, we're coming.

UR'TAMROKOH: Never was a New Year so good.

BEGGAR, SHADOW: Tell us more.

UR'TAMROKOH: They believe and question nothing.

BEGGAR, SHADOW: Poor fools.

UR'TAMROKOH (*slowly as if thinking*): I twist them, twist them and like little bundle put them into my pocket like my father's father's father. No politics new. No politics raw . . . Yes politics cannot blot out strong traditional myths. If you know, you know; (*Walks up and down.*) Keep you Mr Knowing-knowledge in your pocket and get on with what the townsfolks know and want.

SHADOW: You think he is quite well upstairs?

BEGGAR (*beckons Shadow to keep quiet.*) Sssssssiiiiiiihhhhhhhhh.

SHADOW: He will be restless until he has had his New Year's feast of untapped frolickings.

BEGGAR (*mockingly*): The gods will, he doesn't; the Oracle decides; he chooses . . . (*They chuckle.*)

SHADOW: To be Primate of burglars and virgins.

BEGGAR: How old do you think he is?

SHADOW: How old do you think is the Oracle?

BEGGAR: Easy. Try guessing the age of the gods.

SHADOW: What do you think he will die of – stroke?

BEGGAR: Blast, I predict high blood pressure.

SHADOW: Just fancy, a thief can make fools of an entire nation and get the best of everything.

UR'TAMROKOH:
    T'nseecnh oh T'nseecnh oh
    krappo T'nseecnh oh.

BEGGAR: Is he allergic to hay-fever?

SHADOW: He has a big nose. That's why he sneezes so lavishly.

UR'TAMROKOH:
    T'nseecnh oh T'nseecnh oh
    krappo T'nseecnh oh.

SHADOW: Tell him to stuff it up . . .

BEGGAR: Me? Are you mad? Can't you see he is one of those whose madness is incurably mixed with crime. (*Shadow laughs scornfully. Beggar feeling a little embarrassed, decides to face Ur'Tamrokoh. He coughs. With a pompous voice.*) Eh . . . Mr . . . eh Master of the dead, Interpreter of the unknown gods of dogs. Destroyer of Gbakanda virgins and tormentor of peace and rest. Director of night walkers . . .

UR'TAMROKOH:
    T'nseecnh oh T'nseecnh oh
    krappo T'nseecnh oh

SHADOW (*still laughing*): For his gods' and Oracle's sake, please leave him alone or he'll never stop.

BEGGAR: Ur'Tamrokoh of Akpata rocks; twin brother of Gbana-Bendu, shadow of Gbana the Great, leader of all Gbakanda tribe, how fared your mortal men last night in plundering Gbakanda land?

UR'TAMROKOH (*looks around*): Men and beasts must live

in peace. So fools and gods must fair-play well and without
fear.

BEGGAR: The bull, the lion, great ageless mountain of
Gbakandaland, you speak in riddles confusing people.

UR'TAMROKOH: Understand what you will. Misunderstand
not, what you don't.

SHADOW (*confronting him*): Tell us in very simple words; not
in animal tongues, nor in your gods' thoughts and Oracle's
what-not: what's to become of Umu the maid whom you
have trained so well in the art of deception?

BEGGAR: Is she not being wrongly used for the art of crime?

UR'TAMROKOH: The gods will . . . The Oracle decides . . .

BEGGAR: What of the Gbakandas, suppose they are caught?

UR'TAMROKOH: Human beings are made with innate dis-
honesty. Two legged man know destruction proper. You
with five senses know no better. What a shame, what a
waste, what a race. Man, man, man. What are they. So sen-
sitive and sentimental. The world destroys man. Man's societies are destructive to man . . . lives in constant plunder.
Man, oh man. What a shame, what a waste in man's race.
Man; fat man. yellow man, man small, man black, man
red, man big. Punny man black; born in turmoil to perish
in servitude. Funny man white, full of mean spoils,
exploits to no end. Oh yes man. Big man, power man.
How di worl' don spoil, di worl' don spoil. (*He wanders
off. Shadow and Beggar eye each other and follow after him.*)

ACT ONE: SCENE FOUR

*Mid-afternoon of the same day. Gbakanda village. Typically
African with mud-huts, etc. Usually the prominent haunt for
out-of-workers and off-workers. A rendezvous for topical gossips.
A sign-post reads: 'Only Akpeteshe and palm-wine served in
gourds available'. The Beggar and Shadow are sitting opposite
each other on small tree trunks holding bowls of drink. They are
drunk.*

MAMMY-QUEEN (*local proprietor*): When somt'in don pwel, he don' spoil finish.

SHADOW: 'E nor only spoil finish; E foroku.

MAMMY-QUEEN: So I hear Umu is the New Year's sacrifice for Ur'Tamrokoh.

BEGGAR: The gods will it unreservedly for Ur'Tamrokoh.

SHADOW: Which kin' god; damn the thieving idiot. We know what's going on.

MAMMY-QUEEN: Me daddy me don't know oh. Do ya don't come mix me up. I have trade all my grandmothers; I am capable of knowing my own price at an auction.

SHADOW: You are all too backward. That girl is a spot beauty. You sacrifice her to that impotent buffalo who comes telling you that the gods will, will, will my foot.

BEGGAR: Keep your gumption shut. What do you know about the damn thing, ehn? Come on, tell me, god father for chic, chi chi, chickens.

SHADOW: What do you know that I don't know, you un-sober church mouse? To drink like fish and cackle like an old witch – quack, quck, pak, lak, lak, lak, kaka, kak, kak, kak, kak.

BEGGAR: Go on pepper bird, yak, yak, yak, yak, yak. You mouth smell like ogeri kaynda. What you want to tell me that I don't know already?

MAMMY-QUEEN: What kin' palaver this? Who ask you two for take up Gbakandaland New Year case, ehn?

BEGGAR: Just you wait Mammy-Queen. Let him 'Gbarra' people's case . . . Butu-Me-Look; master palaver die quietly for his house; you nosey-parker die disgraceful in the gutter.

SHADOW (*going to Beggar*): Talk one word more. Jes' scoff one more word and see if I nor go skammish you jabbat for you.

BEGGAR (*facing Shadow. He shouts in rather hysterical falsetto voice*): Knack, knack, go on knack. Make you slap me. Here is my face, slap me you are not a man. (*Shadow stands motionless. He finds it all ridiculously funny. Mammy-Queen and people watching begin to laugh at the now very comic situation. Beggar turns and offers his other cheek to Shadow who still stands stupefied*). I give you the other cheek. Knack, come and knack. You and police will decide the rest. Knack, knack. Go on what are you waiting for. Here knack, knack.

(*By this time there are men sitting all about watching and drinking.*)

MAMMY-QUEEN (*Goes up to Beggar and Shadow*): All right. All right. This is not the proper place and time for quarrels and petty misunderstandings. You must leave satan to go his way.

VOICES: New Year is in the air.

Let the old year fade away with its curses and bad luck . . . Disunity brothers, should roll away with the dead and lost of the old year . . .

Brother, una leh we drink and play and laugh together . . . the gods have taken theirs. The Oracle will soon be fulfilled. Let's go gay in our own little way.

SHADOW (*turning away*): Bless these people. If not I would have knocked all your thirty-two out of your 'Yorror' mouth. Scamp.

BEGGAR: What's holding you back? Knack. Here, come knack. Knack.

UR'TAMROKOH (*enters and goes straight to sit on a bamboo stool, bigger and taller than the others*): Fighting is a good sport for Gbakanda hunters, not drunkards with noisy bladders. The wrestler must fight the bull. But only in the arena. Give me Akpeteshe, Mammy-Queen. The air here is cold and the world is growing old outside. All men are losing their sense of reasoning and proportions. In maddening despair they lose face and go wild. What a shame, what a waste, what a race!

MAMMY-QUEEN: Crafty old ageless Ur'Tamrokoh; why is it that the viper has not given birth for so long?

UR'TAMROKOH: When thirteen-year-olds are mothers of triplets, what do you expect?

MAMMY-QUEEN: Wise wizard; lover of darkness, is it true that the gods have willed and the Oracle decided, Gbana-Bendu has trapped his Shadow?

UR'TAMROKOH: Train your eyes to be actively vigilant in observing. Let your mouth speak not too much; but your ears alert like a bat, picking up significant news.

MAMMY-QUEEN: All lizards lay flat on their stomachs.

UR'TAMROKOH: No gynaecologist can tell which one is pregnant and which has constipation . . .

MAMMY-QUEEN: Ur'Tamrokoh!

UR'TAMROKOH: When birds fly past above. I can tell how many eggs they have yet to be hatched, lying patiently in the stomach.

MAMMY-QUEEN: Nar 'im dat. Mana pass man.

UR'TAMROKOH: Believe this or not. When hearts go sore, eyes must shed tears.

MAMMY-QUEEN: Ur'Tamrokoh: business is bad and life is hard.

UR'TAMROKOH: Yan-ka-di, Mammy-Queen. Yan-ka-di.

MAMMY-QUEEN: This is good news. Good news indeed.

SHADOW: The gods decide the inexplicable.

BEGGAR: The Oracle stands indefatigable.

UR'TAMROKOH: My drink, my drink, my liver yearns for hot akpeteshe. (*Mammy-Queen goes off.*) Bad breeze is blowing my direction. Scarcity of perfume and high price on toothpaste.

SHADOW (*insultingly*): Whose favourite virtue is Bigotry?

BEGGAR: His benevolence towards his fellow man, I hear is cheating and stealing of virgins; plundering and killing.

SHADOW: Chief characteristics, they gossip, are single-mindedness. No, No, singleness of purpose.

BEGGAR: Ideas of happiness; lying and perpetuating ignorance, and misery in the name of traditions.

SHADOW: Favourite occupation: womanizing at New Year
with sacrifice most chaste under velvet skin.

BEGGAR: Virtue most appraised. Servility from the ignorant
Gbakandas.

SHADOW: Fool. A big fat fool. Can never jump three foot
pole.

BEGGAR (*to Ur'Tamrokoh*): Sah. You are guilty of conscious
cruelties and inhuman brutalities. What's more you are a
party to night burglary, managing director and organizer
of large-scale thieving.

SHADOW: Baptize him in the name of the most blessed palm-
wine communion. The egregious brute. Kan-Kan doma-
doma, Kan-kan doma-doma. (*Beggar joins him. They
dance very near to Ur'Tamrokoh. The others look on amazed and
quite terrified. Their movements are cynically obscene, staccato.*)
Chun-chun-naam-paelae. Ur'Tamrokoh nam paelae . . .
nam-nam paelae. Chum-chum; pan-chum; pam-pam
paelae . . . Lie man nam-paelae Mammy-Queen nam
paelae . . . mam Ur'Tamrokoh paelae Gbakanda fools,
naam-paelae . . . Gbana-Bendu Shadow paelae. (*They
dance round Ur'Tamrokoh.*) New Year's bride Paelae. Oracle
nam-nam paelae. God's will chun-chun-nam-paelae.
Tamrokoh-paelae. Tamrokoh-Paelae. Tamrokoh-paelae.
(*Mammy-Queen returns with Ur'Tamrokoh's drink. She stops
unable to believe her eyes at what's going on.*)

UR'TAMROKOH: The day has many strange misapprehensions. The night no doubt will flurry the rabbles. Let the
young make fun of grey hairs when they are drunk with
their own piss. Come, the old is already wrinkled, why
do you frown? Give me Akpeteshe. My liver riles within
for the viper poison.

MAMMY-QUEEN: What kin' of wahala trouble-makers are
they?

BEGGAR (*laughs bold and broad*): Thus spake 'fatty-bumpy'
her royal highness, Mammy-Queen. We are wahala
trouble-makers.

SHADOW (*dancing and singing*): Kan-kan doma-doma. Kan-kan doma-doma. Kan-kan doma-doma. Kan-kan doma-doma.

BEGGAR: Maker of Kings and hater of change. Blast, blast, blast.

SHADOW: Now you have had you liver cooled. Sing us the tunes of your great deeds with virgin brides and plundering clans.

MAMMY-QUEEN: Why do you want to cause trouble? Why?

SHADOW: By his deeds you are Mammy-Queen. By our deeds we are trouble-makers.

BEGGAR: Why so quiet grand papa interlocutor? Why not deliberate on your inhuman horrors and terrors. Tell us about New Year's achievements. About the chosen sacrifice Umu; the virgin whose purity must validate the rights of ancestral spirits and decadent traditions. Talk about your Gbakanda exploits.

SHADOW: Exonerate the Gbakandas' legend. How about Jaynet Bundle whose sorcery depopulated the Gbakanda race when she vomited billions of mosquitoes whose bites are known the world over.

BEGGAR: Talk, son of Wonko-wan-Yie. Sing us songs of your crippled father and demi-god uncle Wan-foot Jombie. Enlighten us about their bloody deeds and shameless acts you bloody dog.

SHADOW: Impostor. Make it all nicey, nicey for Mammy-Queen. Another foolish mind.

BEGGAR: Go on, stimulate them for the New Year's night.

SHADOW: Don't forget to urge. Let them appreciate that today's sacrifice is a necessary deception. Symbolic of tomorrow's doomed prosperity and still-born progress. How great and pleasant it must be, to live a sheep in wolve's clothing. Sweet, ehn, to be a King and commoner at the same time. Oracle, gods, Gbana-Bendu Ur'Tamrokoh, all in one big fat slub.

BEGGAR: Oh Ur'Tamrokoh, why are there so many like you? Why? Why, why?

UR'TAMROKOH: Find out as you go along. It's the gods will, not I. The Oracle decides; I obey.

SHADOW: That's all you know.

BEGGAR: How to repeat himself. An effective psychology devised for the unthinking and imperceptive minds around.

UR'TAMROKOH:
T'nseecnh oh T'nseecnh oh
krappo T'nseecnh oh

BEGGAR: Blast, blast, blast you damn sneezing idiot.

SHADOW: They are used to it and to him. Habits die hard . . .

MAMMY-QUEEN (*picks up pestle and chases them out*): Out! I say make you two trouble-makers get out. Out, out, out.

SHADOW (*sings and runs around*): Kan-kan doma-doma. Kan-kan doma doma. Kan-kan doma-doma. Kan-kan doma-doma.

BEGGAR: Damn, blast, blast, blast stupid wretches. I'll come back and that swine will surely repent. Blast, blast, blast.

SHADOW (*going*): Forget the naam doma-doma, forget the naam. Damn.

UR'TAMROKOH:
T'nseecnh oh T'nseecnh
krappo T'nseecnh oh

MAMMY-QUEEN: Who are they? From where do they come? What bad breeze brought them here?

UR'TAMROKOH: The world don spoil bad-bad, Mammy-Queen. Yes, I can see it. I feel it.

MAMMY-QUEEN: The worl' is gettin from bad to worse.

UR'TAMROKOH: Man. What a shame. What a race; what a waste.

(*A slow fade. He slowly downs his drink.*)

ACT TWO: SCENE ONE

The setting is the same as in Act one, scene four. Now there is a group of the village women. Singing harmoniously at the same time looking up and down the road as if expecting someone or something. The time is early evening.

MAMMY-QUEEN (*leads the singing*):

I look; I look; I look.

I see my mother is coming

If you have any gold and silver for me

Save I must be saved.

CHORUS:

No. No. No.

I have no gold and silver

I have no gold and silver for you

Hang must you be hanged.

MAMMY-QUEEN: So her mother could not help. The poor girl sat there crying. It seems as if there was no hope. Time goes past. It was now eating time and her father was making his way home. So she sings to him for help:

(*Sings.*)

I look; I look; I look

I see my father approaching

If you have any gold and silver for me

Save I must be saved.

CHORUS:

No. No. No.

I have no gold and silver

I have no gold and silver for you

Hang must you be hanged.

MAMMY-QUEEN: It is hard when your mother and father turn away from you. When they show no sign of caring; no loving spirit. I would rather be dead than know my parents hate me. Such was the tight-rope of this unfortunate girl who despised her parents and got married

E

to a cretin of a wealthy devil. Her time of death was fast
approaching. The death-clock was ticking away above her
head. Far down the village she espied her brother and
sister. She made her last and desperate cry to the last of
all she'd hope to save her.

I look; I look; I look
I see my brother and sister
If you have any gold and silver for me
Save I must be saved.

CHORUS:
No. No. No.
We have no gold and silver
We have no gold and silver for you
Hang must you be hanged.

(*At this moment a young girl comes rushing in with slippers in
hand. She's followed by other kids carrying such implements as
sticks, pestles, hammers, basket covers. They break the whole
set up. Shouting and ducking and beating the ground with their
various weapons.*)

GIRL:
It is under that bench . . .
Kill am . . . Look, it has gone over there . . .
Go under that bench. Hammer it . . .

CHORUS:
What? Wooops. Ayieeeee. What is it? Drive it away.
Ayieee.

MAMMY-QUEEN: What in God's name is it?

GIRL: A big bush rat ma. It will call snake into the house ma.

MAMMY-QUEEN: You foolish children, get back to your work.
When there is cat in the house, the rat must feel free. Get
back to your work. They are only finding an excuse to
come and spy on what we are doing.

1ST WOMAN: I was enjoying the story, Mammy-Queen.

3RD WOMAN: So was I too.

MAMMY-QUEEN I was just coming to the end.

3RD WOMAN: It is a pathetic story. Very sad.

1ST WOMAN: I felt cramp and cold inside of me.

MAMMY-QUEEN: Well, my dear sisters, God moves in a mysterious way. (*Sighs.*)

1ST WOMAN: His wonders to perform.

MAMMY-QUEEN: The eventful fatal turn of happenings for this arrogant village belle who turned down her parents choice and went away to marry an unknown, unaccepted Prince Charming of a Devil and woman killer was one that lived to baffle even the Devil himself . . .

3RD WOMAN: What happened? Did he?

MAMMY-QUEEN: No. He didn't.

1ST WOMAN: Well!

MAMMY-QUEEN: Her childhood lover, a sailor by trade whom she had long refused to marry heard of her plight.

3RD WOMAN: And?

MAMMY-QUEEN: It was because of her that the poor fellow went to sea. He could not bear the sight of her cavorting about with other men who had money. It nearly killed him to know she was married. But love. Love is unsurpassable. True love is undying.

3RD WOMAN: What happened in the end?

MAMMY-QUEEN: Where was I? Oh yes. The sword of the devil was at the ready to strike. At the last stroke of the death-bell. Devil Prince Charming was waiting impatiently. He loved to see blood when there are no gold and silver. Time was at last running out. The minutes gave way to the seconds . . . Prince Charming sniffed about. Bellowed and growled and rant and raved with the terror and desire of death itself at a battlefield ready to massacre. Suddenly the frightened girl burst out singing tearfully, she had seen someone she could vaguely remember. Someone she hoped for sure would be him and remember. Someone she had decried. It was her impulse that drove her on to call for his help.

3RD WOMAN: And did he come to her rescue?

MAMMY-QUEEN:

I look; I look; I look
I see my lover is coming
If you have any gold and silver for me
Save I must be saved.

CHORUS:

Yes, Yes, Yes
I have some gold and silver
I have some gold and silver for you
Save you must be saved.

1ST WOMAN: Did she marry him in the end?

MAMMY-QUEEN: They lived happily ever after and had many, many children.

1ST WOMAN: But that is all myth. It is not the same as our New Year's sacrifice.

3RD WOMAN: It is one and the same thing. Ours is tradition that we have practiced for generation after generation. Our New Year's sacrifice to the gods and the Oracle is our will and our choice. In the case of the A'nancy story of Mammy-Queen, it was a greedy girl selling herself for worldly riches.

1ST WOMAN: How do you know that we are not selling an innocent girl for superstitious ignorance into slavery and bondage?

(*A slight tense pause among the women. They take in with certain uneasiness what the 1st Woman had said.*)

MAMMY-QUEEN: You may be cleverer than us. But we are older than you. What we talk about is what our parents talked about before us and it is what their parents talked about and believed in. Who are you to come and contradict the elders ehn? It is with us; and will be with us for a long, long time to come. Yes, tonight will be another New Year's night. Like all New Year's Eve, before we have our celebrations in Gbakandaland, Gbakanda Oracle and gods must have their sacrifice. There have been many, many beautiful women who have died in the sea. Died during child birth. Died by witchcraft. By accident. Killed

by their husbands because of jealousy and so on and so
forth. Why then should we pick and pine for one beauty
virgin sacrificed for the good of the land.

4TH WOMAN: Thank heaven I am old and rumple and
ugly.

1ST WOMAN: But, Mammy-Queen.

MAMMY-QUEEN: Yes?

1ST WOMAN (*a little timid*): I don't know.

MAMMY-QUEEN: You don't know what?

1ST WOMAN (*nervously*): I don't know and I do not understand why.

MAMMY-QUEEN: Speak and don't panic. Have you ever
known of a coward Gbakanda?

4TH WOMAN: Never. Not in this world. Speak up.

1ST WOMAN (*sums up courage. But a little choked*): How, I
mean, when and how does the . . . the gods and, well,
Oracle get to agree in choosing the New Year's sacrifice?
And yes, why a virgin? (*They look at her horrified.*)

2ND WOMAN: Blasphemy, blasphemy.

3RD WOMAN: Since when have you heard any Gbakanda
tongue or lip, mouth such impertinent blasphemous
questions? When I ask you sisters of Gbakanda?

1ST WOMAN (*she feels every eye on her with hate*): I . . . I was only
feeling in sympathy for Umu. I know her too well. I feel
sorry –

2ND WOMAN: Sorry! You should be proud of her and rejoice
with the Oracle. My own blood-born sister was before
your time sacrifice to the Oracle of Gbana-Bendu.

4TH WOMAN: We all must be ready to take what comes to
us, whether in bits and pieces or as a whole.

3RD WOMAN: And perform our traditional duties as handed
down to us from the elders.

4TH WOMAN: Customs and traditions must prevail.

2ND WOMAN: And be respected.

1ST WOMAN: I have my doubts.

2ND WOMAN: So you doubt Ur 'Tamrokoh our ancestral

chosen leader? You have no belief in the gods and know no respect for the Oracle?

1 ST WOMAN: You all misunderstand me.

2 ND WOMAN: Ai, so you think –

1 ST WOMAN: Yes; well –

MAMMY-QUEEN: Explain yourself child.

1 ST WOMAN: I have my doubts as to the capacity of my strength and weakness. It bothers me as I do not understand yet how much I can sustain and how long I can endure. It is a self-inflicted torture.

MAMMY-QUEEN: How you mean?

1 ST WOMAN: By indulging in self-pity and curiosity. (*Bursts out.*) It feels embarrassing to want to know why this and that happens.

4 TH WOMAN: Especially when you are among us, ehn. Sisters take note.

1 ST WOMAN: I didn't blame it on anyone. I burn inside not being able to understand what happens after. I am lacking and all so empty and lost. I feel like changing places with Umu. Perhaps I might be able to fulfil my curiosity and satisfy the emptiness in me.

2 ND WOMAN: Blasphemous. May Krifi bridle your flippant tongue.

1 ST WOMAN: I heard two men talking about Ur 'Tamrokoh, the Gbakandas' Oracle and gods this morning at the market-place. They frighten me.

2 ND WOMAN: How?

1 ST WOMAN: They talked a lot and I am always frightened of people who talk a lot.

4 TH WOMAN: Empty barrels make the most noise.

1 ST WOMAN: These are not barrels, they are men and look real. They talk about what they've seen here in Gbakanda-land. They are strangers not from too far a country. I think Obasai. So they sound. But they know Ur 'Tamrokoh, and they talk about him and things I dare not say here.

2 ND WOMAN: Why not?

ST WOMAN (*abruptly*): Nothing. I don't know . . . Don't ask me.

MAMMY-QUEEN: These two strangers you talk about came here early in the day. They talked a lot. Plenty of unusual nastiness about them –

ND WOMAN: Strangers are always full of rubbish.

MAMMY-QUEEN: I chased them out good and proper.

TH WOMAN: Now child; my dear child, let not the evil talks of idle tongues confuse your mind and break your heart. We came into this world before you. We were saluted by the sun, and moon and stars before you. So we know what we are talking about. We cannot deceive you. We are your guides, your advisers and elders. Look on us and believe in what we believe. Follow in our footsteps and you will never take a wrong step. Ur 'Tamrokoh is our father of fathers. Our protector. Our redeemer. The gods chose him and the Oracle blessed him. He is first and last. Without him, we are not. With him, we are what we are. Child, dear child, believe and trust in the devil you know: never risk your faith in outrageous soothsayers like 'Stranger-Saviours'.

HORUS: Amen. So let it be.

RD WOMAN: I think it's about time we set off to see the Sacrifice go.

TH WOMAN: I am always intrigued by it . . . So wonderful . . . So great . . .

AMMY-QUEEN: Yes. Oh yes. Let's be off. It is no baby distance from here to the Great Gbakanda gates . . . I want to see Umu go.

TH WOMAN: We might as well get started. My legs are not as strong and able as they used to be in the good old days. How I would have liked to dance into the Gbakanda crowd tonight.

ND WOMAN: We will all get to be like you sooner or later.

TH WOMAN: In time, I hope. We all have to wait for our turn.

MAMMY-QUEEN: The gods know best. We wait for their
  decisions.
2ND WOMAN: What they will, we obey. What they decide,
  we accept.
CHORUS: Yan-Ka-di ba-ba. Yan-ka-di.

ACT TWO: SCENE TWO

Night. A deserted street, untarred. The scene is as in Act one, scene
  one. Po-Joe, father of Umu, worn out, walks up and down the
  road. The Beggar and Shadow follow behind him. It seems
  they have been having a go at him for quite a while.

PO-JOE: Tradition is like going to school. Our tradition i
  like going to school. The Gbakanda Secret Society Bush
  is in fact a school.
BEGGAR: I see.
PO-JOE: We do exactly as we are told.
SHADOW: Perfect. Don't do as I do, but do as I tell you.
BEGGAR: Don't interrupt Po-Joe. He is trying to excuse him
  self to us for the poor and ridiculous state in which he i
  in –
SHADOW: And will always be in.
PO-JOE: You two are real strangers. You can never under
  stand us.
BEGGAR: We are already standing under.
SHADOW: Perfectly perfect.
PO-JOE: I hope you will be in perfect conditions to join u
  in our New Year's Eve Celebrations.
SHADOW, BEGGAR: That's exactly why we are here. Hav
  no doubts about that.
BEGGAR: Will the gods and the Oracle be present to receiv
  their human sacrifice at the Celebrations?
PO-JOE: Always. But Invisible.
SHADOW: Just like our God.
BEGGAR: It is a shame you have so many gods plus a
  Oracle. We have only one.

SHADOW: You might as well ask why some men have one wife and others twenty and more.

BEGGAR: Primitive backwardness, I call it.

SHADOW (*shouts*): Hey, hey, look; just look over there. Umu the sacrifice heads the crowd.

BEGGAR: She's walking as if she's drunk a dozen jugs of palm wine.

PO-JOE (*to himself. Very grieved*): Oh you gods! We know that from the days of the great Tonko-Baelae master tongue-twister, no one has dared to refuse the Oracle's wish. Who am I, little Po-Joe, to defy the gods' will, the Oracle's wish? Who am I? Why should I desire an unprosperous New Year when others before me have yielded willingly?

BEGGAR: What are your gains for giving your only daughter away to be sacrificed?

PO-JOE: You are not of us. You won't understand –

SHADOW: For self-esteem and status?

PO-JOE: You strangers are tired. It confuses your way of thinking.

BEGGAR: Will you achieve a position of power?

PO-JOE: To hell with you two and stop your gnashing at me. Go!

SHADOW: Can you hear what they are saying? The crowd –

VOICES (*from a distance*):
Here she comes.
Daughter of Akriboto
Child of Okobo.

BEGGAR: Be a Gbakanda strong and proud. Refuse the Oracle for once.

PO-JOE: Impossible, blasphemy, impossible. It is sabotage what you suggest.

BEGGAR: Not impossible! Tell that thief Ur 'Tamrokoh he is a thief and he can go to hell with his gods and Oracle.

PO-JOE: May the gods forgive what you just said. (*Firmly.*) Look my good friends, do not interfere with our way of life. You will be pushing yourselves into bad trouble. My daughter Umu believes in what she is doing. I do. We all do. You can't change it. We can't change it. We are used to this way of life. If you ask us to change, what can you give us in place of this? What do you think will make us happy and please us, that we can put all our faith, hope and trust in? My friends, my daughter Umu belongs where the gods are. I don't know you. And you don't mean anything to me, nor to my fellow Gbakandas. You are like Harmattan wind. Temporary visitors, wanting to disturb and upset everything. Why?

BEGGAR: See! The man has got good motives. His daughter is to go with the Squares. She is too good for the likes of us. Drunks and beggars, bums and tramps.

PO-JOE (*hatefully*): Go away you despicable drunks and leave me alone. (*The crowd draws near, the noise becomes clearer.*) Let me do my duties to my elders, the dead and my ancestors. Go, go, go back to where you come from. (*The crowd surrounds Beggar, Shadow and Umu and Po-Joe.*)

UMU (*as if in distress*): Father. Father. (*Gbakanda women and men watch with interest.*)

PO-JOE: I know you not. You are not of my loins. Never.

UMU: I go, Father. I am the eclipsed child. The dark-night bride. I am Umu, the orphan maid married to a man whose face they tell is black dark night of Johnson-Spring. Gbana-Bendu, my man, my husband, my master, my love. I am on my way. Tonight is the night of the Vestal virgins.

CHORUS: Oh unfortunate thighs that will know no warmth of nervous clutchings!

UMU (*spoken, not sung*):
No music at my wedding
No dancing, drinking and singing
No libation, no garlands
No crown for the new queen of Gbana-Bendu.

CHORUS:
Never a crown for uncircumcised queens

not for you, Umu, never has been
Not in Gbakandaland. No, Umu, not here.

BEGGAR (*to the women*): Do you all despise her? Or is it the usual precedent and custom of the gods and Oracle? Oh you fallen remains of Gbakanda. On your invitations your gods make their visitations. Oh you hypocrites. You bar your doors and lock your windows against simple human beings. You shut your eyes against progress and change. At nights, your unclean minds shake with fear, your hearts of stone go jelly and wobble at the simple rattle on your door-locks by gentle winds. You go all panic twitching. The buzzing of the bumble-bee confuses your speech. Much less, the bite of a mosquito makes you angry with little children. Oh little scandalous women. What are your memories of yesterday's pleasures? What are your feelings of today's 'Strange Misapprehensions' and shame? What will be the cause of your fears for tomorrow's dangers?

UR'TAMROKOH (*they make way for him*): The evil shadows are still with us. What a pity Gbakanda's sons are travelling far and fast. There is so much on hand to do.

SHADOW: Like breaking into houses at this very hour when all the homes are deserted by these busy-bodies and ignorant layabouts who haven't the faintest idea how much you have planned to plunder them, good and proper.

4TH WOMAN (*with venom*): Oh womb that bore forth so many Gbakandas, how I wish for my sons to be here. They would strike you down never to rise again; you untrained and uncouth wretch.

SHADOW (*with a rebuff*): Go call them then wherever they may be. I can wait.

MAMMY-QUEEN: Idiot. In what womb were you conceived and nurtured?

SHADOW: In a woman's of course. But not like the likes of you.

4TH WOMAN: Oh unhappy mother that I am. Four sons

alive and strong, yet I live to be rudely insulted by drunken beggars.

UMU: Had I a mother to grieve for me, how easy my burden would have been.

BEGGAR: It is never too late.

UR'TAMROKOH:
T'nseecnh oh T'nseecnh oh
krappo T'nseecnh oh

UMU (*to Po-Joe*): Father help me. Come with me.

PO-JOE (*he moves away*): Touch me not you accursed leper. (*As he moves away, Umu misses her grip. She falls flat on her face and stays there.*)

UR'TAMROKOH:
T'nseecnh oh T'nseecnh oh
krappo T'nseecnh oh

SHADOW (*gestingly*): Now the Oracle must be fulfilled.

UR'TAMROKOH:
T'nseecnh oh T'nseecnh oh
krappo T'nseecnh oh

PO-JOE: Yan-ka-di ba-ba

MAMMY-QUEEN: The gods will soon be pleased.

4TH WOMAN: New Year's harvest will be rich.

2ND WOMAN: True say talk me; she's the most beautiful, most charming and most elegant of all the maiden sacrifices I have seen in my own time.

MAMMY-QUEEN: Say that again oh.

4TH WOMAN: True. Quite true.

3RD WOMAN: Umu is a beautiful girl.

1ST WOMAN: The Oracle and the gods must have good taste and such palpable appetite.

SHADOW: I envy them.

UR'TAMROKOH:
T'nseecnh oh T'nseecnh oh
krappo T'nseecnh oh

PO-JOE:
Yan-ka-di

Ba-ba.

UMU (*looks around*): The orphan is quite ready to be taken away and be made an offering to the gods and the Oracle.

CHORUS: A very special sacrifice. New Year's especial sacrifice.

PO-JOE:
Yan-ka-di ohhhhhhhhhhhh
Yan-ka-di.

1ST WOMAN (*To Umu*): Sister of sorrow and shame; friend of woe and disgrace; Umu, enemy to light and right, I wish I could come to befriend the darkness with you. To sit and wait without hope and leave them with their New Year full of bliss.

UMU: Thank you, thank you sister of sympathy. The fingers point hard on me. My path is a lone winding one. I alone pick my way. No help, no love, no friend.

UR'TAMROKOH:
T'nseecnh oh T'nseecnh oh
krappo T'nseecnh oh.

2ND WOMAN: Serves you right, sister most sympathetic.

UR'TAMROKOH: A well-choosen sacrifice. The gods know best. The Oracle chooses well. Our sacrifice rids us of all the evils of the past year.

CHORUS: The old gives away to the new. The end becomes infinitesimal, the beginning rekindles a good feeling of youth.

PO-JOE:
Yan-ka-di Ba-ba
Yan-ka-di.

SHADOW: Why don't you protest? Demonstrate to show you disapprove rather than stand there and mumble that belching mumbo-jumbo.

CHORUS: Come let us worship our dead ancestors through our most sacred Oracle. Let us sing the praise of our gods and wait their blessings through Ur 'Tamrokoh our father of fathers.

BEGGAR: You people are potty. You sure have a long way to go and a lot to learn.

SHADOW: They'll never get anywhere. Never.

CHORUS: We will go now to make ready for the New Year's Eve festivity.

SHADOW: Go where? Aren't you going to see the end of your New Year's sacrifice?

2ND WOMAN: You strangers want to teach us our own customs?

BEGGAR: No. But don't you want to see Umu sacrificed? Surely this is not the end. Not what we expect – or is it so bad that you can't be bothered to wait and see it all go through?

SHADOW: What about your sons and husbands? Where are they now? Are they not coming to the sacrificial ceremony?

BEGGAR: Please do not misunderstand our over interestedness and concern. It is all because things look so inhumanly strange to us. We are curious.

SHADOW: Do not worry about our humbugging presence. It is so where we come from. Everyone behaves like us in God forsaken Obasai.

UR'TAMROKOH:
T'nseecnh oh T'nseecnh oh
krappo T'nseecnh oh

CHORUS: We go to complete the gods' desires. To wait in mourning our sons' and husbands' return.

PO-JOE: Yan-ka-di.

CHORUS: We return to the extinguished fireside where no food will be cooked, no water boiled until our sons and husbands return. No mouth will eat food, drink water or talk gossips till our husbands and sons return. Naked as we were born into this world, we go to mingle with ash, dirt and cowdung.

4TH WOMAN: For as we are now, we have fallen into rancour with the uninitiated. We have moved with the accursed.

MAMMY-QUEEN: We must be purified to live with the initiated and partake of Gbakanda's New Year's feast.

UR'TAMROKOH: Humble sisters of Gbakanda let those who know the strangers' wisdom speak loudest. Those who know not plead excuses of their ignorance through their gods and Oracle.

PO-JOE:
Yan-Ka-di
Ba-ba.

SHADOW: You irritate my nerves with your mumble mumbo jumbo.

(*Umu, who was lying on the ground like a heap of dirty clothes, suddenly springs up. She seems to have more life in her. Just as when she challenged the four Gbakandas. She calls out to the women.*)

UMU: Gbakanda women, Gbakanda women, no man in the house –

CHORUS: Yes, there are no men in the house.

UMU: There will be no children –

CHORUS: When there's no man in the house.

UMU: There will be hunger –

CHORUS: When there's no man in the house.

UMU: There will be advantage –

CHORUS: When there's no man in the house.

UMU: Who will help you in times of sickness?

CHORUS: When there's no man in the house.

UMU: Who will warm you when you are old and cold?

CHORUS: When there's no man in the house.

UMU: Who will pay your bride price?

CHORUS: When there's no man in the house.

UMU: Who will carrry your Kassankay?

CHORUS: When there's no man in the house.

UMU: Why must girls be virgins?

CHORUS: When there's no man in the house.

UMU: Why brand women sterile?

CHORUS: When there's no man in the house.

umu: What happiness can a woman have alone?

chorus: When there's no man in the house.

shadow (*gallantly comes forward again. Beggar stays in the background. They both have a bottle of palm-wine in their hands*): Is that the only problem? Man palaver. (*They all look up at him as if awaking from a trance.*)

beggar (*a little cowed*): Male scarcity, that's their economic problem.

ur'tamrokoh:
T'nseecnh oh T'nseecnh oh
krappo T'nseecnh oh.
When trouble does not come your way, never try, never persist in tempting trouble.

shadow: You look so damn conspicuous in that outfit. (*To Beggar.*) Come here quick. (*He comes hurriedly, Shadow whispers to him, he looks around speculatively then assumes an authoritative air.*)

beggar: My master, the Great Chief of Yanda-Yanda (*Pointing to no definite direction.*) would like to speak to you all on, eme, eh, this ridiculous New-Moon-Year celebrations.

ur'tamrokoh:
T'nseecnh oh T'nseecnh oh
krappo T'nseecnh oh
(*Beggar recedes his steps frighteningly.*)

shadow (*to U'Tamrokoh*): If by sneezing you think you can frighten us you are making a fool of yourself. Now you fool (*to Beggar*), what would you do in a country where there are Borku-borku, more women than men? Like in this instance.

beggar: Marry as many as possible.

shadow: Where have you lost your christian 'One man, One wife' monogamy?

beggar: I always carry it around with me, Sah.

shadow: Now, what will you do with all these sex-starved women?

BEGGAR: Well, I don't really know. But I should expect that our friend here would have some fitted excuse in their parables like for instance, 'even dirty water can quench a blazing fire'.

SHADOW: You speak well. Well indeed.

BEGGAR: As long as they are not my brother's wife.

SHADOW: Count adultery out.

BEGGAR: Look at that Angel darling Umu sprawled on dear mother earth.

SHADOW: What a virgin. Oh how the gods and Oracle know what's best to choose.

BEGGAR: What's a virgin?

SHADOW: A young untouched and untapped palm-tree (*as if in ecstasy*), tender, fair and chaste ha-ha . . .

BEGGAR (*jumps in the air*). Ehn, wow-wow. (*Rubs his hands.*) I yie-yie (*He goes to Umu.*)

PO-JOE: Touch her not. She is a leper.

BEGGAR (*eagerly sensual*): Where, where? (*Amorously.*) Let me be contaminated. Let me be a leper. Let me, Umu. Let me, you gods and Oracle. Let me be a leper.

4TH WOMAN: What manner of strangers are these?

SHADOW: Men of action.

MAMMY-QUEEN: What kind of creatures are you?

BEGGAR: Mundane.

2ND WOMAN: Go back to your place of origin. Go, go away to your civilized human Obasai.

CHORUS: Go and take her with you. New Year is here and we want no curse on our soil. We want to reap a good harvest. We want our sons and husbands back. (*The Beggar and Shadow move about and among them as if they are controlling the whole show. They laugh in their faces and touch them without being afraid.*)

BEGGAR (*to Ur'Tamrokoh*): Snee-snoor oh Snee-snoor. (*Jesting.*) Krappo snee-snoor. You sneeze too much. That's why you don't grow. (*To Po-Joe*) Who born dog?

SHADOW: Dog.

BEGGAR: Who born dog?

SHADOW: Dog. (*They quicken the tempo.*)

BEGGAR: Who born dog?

SHADOW: Dog.

BEGGAR: Who born dog?

SHADOW: Dog.

BEGGAR: Who born you? (*Points to Ur 'Tamrokoh.*)

SHADOW: Dog. (*They laugh at Ur 'Tamrokoh.*)

UR'TAMROKOH:
    T'nseecnh oh T'nseecnh oh
    Krappo T'nseecnh oh.

SHADOW (*throws away his empty bottle*): If you sneeze once more I'll arrest you for disturbing the peace and causing public nuisance.

UR'TAMROKOH (*defiantly*):
    T'nseecnh oh T'nseecnh oh
    Krappo T'nseecnh oh.

SHADOW: I see you are trying to be difficult ehn? You don't realize we have taken over, do you. We will soon declare martial law.

4TH WOMAN: Disease and shame; death in disgrace follows behind those who show disrespect to Ur 'Tamrokoh the Great One of Gbakanda land.

BEGGAR: Stop your cackling, old babbler.

SHADOW: She is daft. They are all clothed in darkness. Fools. (*Shouts in disgust.*) Fools all of you. Look at them. They know their genesis. But only he, the crafty geni, Ur 'Tamrokoh, he alone can read them their lamentation and reveal to them their Revelations.

BEGGAR: They have lived in constant fear under his code of Hitlerite dogma.

SHADOW: Stop being afraid.

UMU (*looks up*): Afraid! (*She bursts out laughing.*)

2ND WOMAN: Take her away, she is not of us anymore.

4TH WOMAN: She is possessed by the devil.

3RD WOMAN: She is a barren tree. Rootless and fruitless. Take her away.

MAMMY-QUEEN: Tree without branch. Take her, take her, take her.

BEGGAR: We will when we are ready.

UMU: Am not coming with you, am not of your race; besides there will be no Gbakanda man in the house sisters of Gbakanda.

CHORUS: Yes. There will be no man in the house.

2ND WOMAN: We are happy with no man in the house.

CHORUS: Except Gbakanda man.

4TH WOMAN: We are content with no man in the house.

CHORUS: We are content with no man in the house.

BEGGAR: This is pretty frustrating. How long do you think they can go on without it?

SHADOW: As long as the gods will and the Oracle stands undecided and unchallenged.

UR'TAMROKOH: You are bent on destroying our festivity are you?

SHADOW: We are not. All we want is to prove you and your Oracle and your gods wrong. To help you and these ignorant people . . .

2ND WOMAN: Krifi dislodge his contemptuous tongue. And may your lips hang as heavy as lead.

BEGGAR: To hell and damnation with you and your Krifi. We are talking on your behalf, you go on heaping curses on us.

MAMMY-QUEEN: We don't know you. We don't need you.

SHADOW: We are strangers to you. Yes! But we don't want you to feel strange towards us.

UR'TAMROKOH: Very condescending indeed.

BEGGAR: We know about you so well, you'll be surprised.

SHADOW: Our way and your ways are not the same. But that is no problem . . .

BEGGAR: We are all one and the same now.

SHADOW: Yes, we are the same people.

UR'TAMROKOH:
T'nseecnh oh T'nseecnh oh
Krappo T'nseecnh oh

BEGGAR: Can't you stop this damn ritual sneezing? Soon, you will irritate my hickuping. (*He hickups.*) See what I mean?

SHADOW (*like a preacher*): You people of Gbakanda, Gbakanda people, if you have ears to hear, hear us. We are here to deliver you. To do only one thing for you. It will be a fine thing for us as it will for you.

UR'TAMROKOH: We have been able to do everything for ourselves before you came.

SHADOW (*ignoring Ur'Tamrokoh*): We are not men of greatness; of books and all wisdom like the great Ur'Tamrokoh. But (*pointing to Umu*) that woman there, Umu, it is her we have come to rescue from this your savagery.

UR'TAMROKOH:
T'nseecnh oh T'nseecnh oh
Krappo T'nseecnh oh.

SHADOW (*gasps exasperated*): But before we claim her, because you have all disowned her.

BEGGAR: Even my friend Po-Joe here denies his own belly-born daughter.

SHADOW: Before we take her away I first have one great ritual to perform. Our God demands it and my friend and I have decided.

CHORUS: Perform it. Perform it now and take her away.

BEGGAR: Excellent. You are exceedingly the most generous, most hospitable of all people. Long live your kindly race.

SHADOW (*calmly*): Women of Gbakanda –

4TH WOMAN: On with your ritual.

SHADOW: Ur'Tamrokoh the great all rounder and Po-Joe –

UR'TAMROKOH:
T'nseecnh oh T'nseecnh oh
Krappo T'nseecnh oh

SHADOW: I hope you will be patient with me and listen to

us carefully. As you see, we are of a civilized nature. We need not waste our breath on that. However, our minds are highly cultivated and we are a developed people who have come to show you the light and help you change from your backwardness and develop into something of the universal present.

BEGGAR: History has proved your race as we now find you. Yet we have decided to sacrifice all our comforts, wealth and happiness to come and help you. To drag you out of your mess . . .

UR'TAMROKOH:

T'nseecnh oh T'nseecnh oh.

Krappo T'nseecnh oh

SHADOW: You will make a good time-keeper Ur'Tamrokoh. Now, we are here to take Umu away from being sacrificed. To save her from the harem of the gods' castle and the slavery of the Oracle.

2ND WOMAN: May a vulture pluck out your vile tongue this very minute.

SHADOW: Thank you. It seems you people do not want to hear all that I have to tell and do. Your faces have grown heavy and dark and hard with bitterness. Maybe it is going to rain and it seems we have been holding too long, preventing Ur'Tamrokoh to go ahead with the customary ceremony. Well we might as well get to the point. Have you ever seen a topless woman?

BEGGAR: They'll run in doors and lock themselves in for seven days and nights praying to their gods and Oracle for purification.

SHADOW: What about introducing them to the mini-minus-minor?

BEGGAR: You must be out of your mind. The gods will order a grand scale arrest for the Oracle to feast all New Year, Christmas, Easter, Whitsun and Rahmadan. Sacrifices of legs most varied and most appetizing, oh yes!

SHADOW: What about striptease?

BEGGAR: Gbakandaland will surely be struck down with the worst of epidemics, especially coronary thrombosis and stroke.

UR'TAMROKOH:
T'nseecnh oh T'nseecnh oh
Krappo T'nseecnh oh.

SHADOW (*eyes Ur'Tamrokoh. Sarcastically*): Yes, of course. I'll proceed with the ritual. (*To Po-Joe.*) Now you will agree that Umu is your daughter!

PO-JOE: I know her not.

SHADOW: But you know her mother well, ehn?

BEGGAR (*attempts to strike Po-Joe*): Answer you inhuman stoop.

SHADOW: Don't hit him. Pull the girl up. (*Slowly.*) Nice and easy, untie her wrapper.

PO-JOE (*shouts pleadingly*): No! No! No! Not before my eyes. Please Ur'Tamrokoh, stop them. Stop him. It is the worst of all the curses for a . . . a . . .

SHADOW: But why? We are only performing our own strangers' New Year ritual to which you all agreed.

BEGGAR: She is not your daughter, her nakedness should not embarrass you.

PO-JOE: I swear to you that she is not my daughter. I swear I know her not.

UR'TAMROKOH:
T'nseecnh oh T'nseecnh oh
Krappo T'nseecnh oh.

SHADOW: Sneeze more Ur'Tamrokoh. Sneeze, you can't stop us now. You can't.

BEGGAR (*Pulls Umu up*): Look at me. I am human. We are different. Have you heard the saying? 'There's something behind two which makes three so cooked.' Do you know?

UMU: Yes, oddness –

BEGGAR: Odd things are evil. Give an odd person power and he'll abuse, misuse and destroy. We, my friend and I, we always go even, to make things just . . .

HADOW (*shouts*): I say strip her, not speak her.

O-JOE: I must go home. The gods have plagued this ritual. The Oracle has undone Po-Joe for life. I am sick. Death is my only consoler.

HADOW (*to Po-Joe*): You go nowhere without our God's will and our permission.

O-JOE (*protesting*): I can't stay here to see this blasphemy.

HORUS: We must not stay here any longer to see the evil hands of the gods descend and destroy.

HADOW: Krifi will follow you all to your huts and shacks and hunt you down. Your gods will spit upon you angrily and so will your Oracle bring you to utter ruin and annihilation for desertion in the most trying time.

R'TAMROKOH: You yap like fishmongers, boast like eunuchs trying to bed pregnant prostitutes. How fearful you bark, you toothless hounds.

HADOW: If we bark, we bite. A dangerous bite that will be your disgrace. Our poison is potent and can destroy you for ever.

EGGAR: Your people of Gbakanda will disown you if we bite. Like you who have destroyed many of their kith and kin in the name of archaic traditions, so will they devour you and make a burnt sacrifice out of you.

R'TAMROKOH: As you threaten me, so will the gods deliver you for unmerciful destruction –

EGGAR (*sarcastically*): And the Oracle will anoint you in evil devices.

HADOW (*commandingly*): Now strip her. (*Beggar forcefully pulls off Umu's wrapper. She stands gracefully clad in black bra and corset and black under-pants. Po Joe falls flat on his face. The women wail agonizingly covering their eyes.*)

HORUS: Krifi oh Krifi. Krifi has come into Gbakandaland. Ur'Tamrokoh save us from this sin and shame.

(*Ur'Tamrokoh looks on unmoved but full of anger.*)

HADOW: Shut up you malnutrited lazy foggies. You ju-ju worshippers. You know of nothing beyond your

Gbakanda parochialism. You live for nothing but prayer
in patience for Hope, Faith and Charity. Look at her.
Look at her beauty, the woman you are giving away as
sacrifice. (*Pulls Po-Joe up strongly.*) Now ask her forgiveness
Go on, look at her. Take her all in, you bum of a father.

BEGGAR: She is only human. You can see her, touch her
and taste her, if you like . . . eh. But you can't with your
Oracle.

UR'TAMROKOH: My friends what are you trying to do
Tell us, what are you trying to prove? Don't you know
that all this same liberality, open mindedness, truth and
unconventions of ideas and approach and mannerisms
have all been attempted and tried as effectively but without success by more greater and influential and powerful
men than you?

BEGGAR: That's exactly why they failed. For like you,
Ur'Tamrokoh, those men had greatness and power trust
upon them by confounded idiots. Those idiots, like these,
gave all their support with absolute faith and implicit
beliefs. Unlike you and those great and powerful men, we
are here not to show by demonstration our power or
greatness. We have neither. We don't seek after them
either. All we want to see is truth and justice practised.
Not for you to get all the juicy and best, and they collect
the crumbs over which some of them die because of the
long waiting and scrambling in the last minute.

UR'TAMROKOH (*going*): If you tarry with us you will see
what will come to pass before your very eyes. I go now.

SHADOW (*stops him*): You don't leave until we say so.

BEGGAR: This time your gods don't will you and your
Oracle won't decide. Now your fate hangs on our scale.
We are in the middle of the process of balancing it. Well
and proper. We want you to tell us why it is only you who
should be so privileged and fortunate to be the almighty
and unquestionable father of all Gbakanda. The great
infallible one.

CHORUS: Trouble oh trouble. Trouble like A'nancy story has fallen on us all. Gbakanda is shaken; the dead are raging.

SHADOW: The dead are dead, so they cannot rage. It is you who are hearing yourselves raging. Woe unto the conceit of undeveloped minds. This devil you all so well worship; this deformed minded ape you all so greatly respect is nothing but an old odd trickster.

2ND WOMAN: We thank you for that. Go and leave us in peace.

BEGGAR: You must believe us. You must trust us.

SHADOW: We are going to expose some of his shrewd and discreet accomplishments which has kept you so backward for a whole millennium. (*Taking Umu by the cheeks.*) First, let me kiss her and become a leper.

BEGGAR (*with great efforts he kisses Umu's hand*): I too will endeavour to do the same. Two is friend, three is company. (*He kisses her hand, twice and then three times.*) She is wonderfully soft. Here. (*Gives her the wrapper.*) Now you will not be lonely and cold and unhappy.

CHORUS: There are men in the house but not Gbakanda men.

SHADOW: That's why Ur'Tamrokoh sends them out thieving. Why don't you ask him what usually happens to some of your men when they go to the secret society bush and do not return and they are never heard of –

UR'TAMROKOH (*raising his stick to hit Shadow*): Death will be your recompense, I promise you.

BEGGAR (*grabbing the stick*): Never fight with a weapon, especially when there are no Gbakandas in the house.

4TH WOMAN: Trouble oh trouble in the land of Gbakanda.

SHADOW (*dodging in and out of the crowd*): Don't pit your chronic strength against me Ur'Tamrokoh, Gbanda-Bendu.

UMU (*mock surprise*): So, so you, you Ur'Tamrokoh, you are Gbana-Bendu. Yes, yes, it's true. Love they say is blind . . .

BEGGAR: Man among men. Ur 'Tamrokoh surnamed Gbana-Bendu . . .

UR'TAMROKOH:
T'nseecnh oh T'nseecnh oh
Krappo T'nseecnh oh.

PO-JOE (*bewildered*): Ur 'Tamrokoh!

SHADOW: Answer the man. Tell your folks about their sacrifice daughters. What happens to them after New Year. Tell why it is always necessary for you alone to take the sacrifices to the out of town shrine and make the offering alone and by night. Tell them why it is only at New Year that thieving is always so rampant and concentrated.

BEGGAR: Why don't you speak King of thieves, lecherer of virgins, harbourer of a thousand and one wives kept as slaves.

PO-JOE: Gbakanda child, a slave?

BEGGAR: Far worse than our civilized prostitutes.

SHADOW: Let him take you to his royal palace. What he calls the out of town Shrine.

BEGGAR: Have any of you been there?

1ST WOMAN: No. Never. Never.

BEGGAR: Why?

1ST WOMAN: It is forbidden to the circumcised and initiated.

BEGGAR: Why?

1ST WOMAN: We never asked. Not allowed to question.

CHORUS: It is forbidden. Ur 'Tamrokoh knows best.

PO-JOE: Questions are unasked in Gbakandaland.

UR'TAMROKOH
T'nseecnh oh T'nseecnh oh
Krappo T'nseecnh oh.

BEGGAR: Ask for forgiveness or we shall finish you off. We have exhibits of your slow annihilation of the Gbakanda people.

UR'TAMROKOH: Maybe you should also start stripping me as you've done her and see what will become of you.

SHADOW: You threaten us!

CHORUS: Who are they? Why have you come to disrupt our lives and upset the normal flow of things? From what hole, under what stone, what sea and what hiding did you get the nerves and courage and news which brought you here?

PO-JOE: We don't want you here.

4TH WOMAN: Who sent you here?

SHADOW: The all merciful Saviour sent us to rescue you.

3RD WOMAN: You say we are one. But you also tell us that we live in the valley of the shadow of darkness.

BEGGAR: Yet you fear goodness and prefer evil.

UR'TAMROKOH:

T'nseecnh oh T'nseecnh oh
Krappo T'nseecnh oh.

As long as I am alive and living with them, they will go by what the gods will and the Oracle decides. I will be their guide and carry their staff. They will have the comfort and happiness they are used to having. Their faith will grow and their hope and trust in me will not falter. Destroy me; you annihilate them. Trying to convince them to distrust me is like trying without faith to move mountains. They know no other ways but this. My ways and my fathers' ways. So it will be. Generation after generation yet unborn will accept my ways without questions. They will accept no other way but my way.

BEGGAR: You are the impregnable, the indefatigable. Mighty indestructable Ur'Tamrokoh, Gbana-Bendu.

SHADOW (*to Umu*): Come, you sweet darling angel of brown clay. You virgin of the wild jungle. Come go with me and I'll teach you my ways. I will love you as my equal. Like a woman should be loved.

UMU (*without moving*): Love is blind. I love this way. I prefer this Gbakanda way and love Ur'Tamrokoh's ways.

SHADOW: But they are backward and primitive. This is no place for you. I am offering you the riches any woman could ever pray for.

UMU: But this is my place. My fate. My home. In life or death. In disgrace and in shame. No place else is good for me but Ur'Tamrokoh's place. (*Shadow pulls and tugs Umu. She resists. Finally she hits him, he falls to the ground and the women boo and jeer at Shadow. Ur'Tamrokoh smiles in triumph.*) Can't you understand? Leave me. Leave us alone. Go, go, go before the bad crowd swallows you up and destroys you.

SHADOW: They are heathens.

BEGGAR: They are grown slaves, believers of human sacrifice.

SHADOW (*to Umu*): They will destroy you. They hate you Umu.

BEGGAR: We know it. We heard him say so.

UMU: Thank you; but please go away before they turn their anger on you. Leave us, leave us please. Go, go, go.

SHADOW: But, but we can't leave you here to die – we can't.

BEGGAR (*pleading*): We have a better home and you will have a better life.

SHADOW: Our streets have shining lights sparkled with diamonds; our houses are built on high hills overlooking the blue seas. Come with us, please.

(*Umu breaks away into the crowd and runs off.*)

UMU: Go away. Leave us as we are. Go, go, go.

(*They go after her.*)

BEGGAR AND SHADOW: Umu come back. Come go with us. Umu please come with us. Come go with us. Come. Come.

2ND WOMAN: They are mad.

3RD WOMAN: Who are they?

4TH WOMAN: From where have they come?

CHORUS: Who sent them? Who asked them?

UR'TAMROKOH:

T'nseecnh oh T'nseecnh oh
Krappo T'nseecnh oh.
The gods will, not I:

The Oracle decides, I obey.

Umu has gone, gone, gone, but not lost from the Oracle.

PO-JOE:

Yan-ka-di

Ba-ba.

UR'TAMROKOH: She will be met by the strong arms of the ancestors. (*Relieved.*) Now, New Year is fast approaching again. There will be much rejoicing. Plenty to eat, to drink and dance. We are the same people. Always the same. Always have been. Always will be. You have proved your faith.

2ND WOMAN: We know what is good for us.

PO-JOE: We know and believe it through and through.

3RD WOMAN: We are the only people of Gbakanda.

4TH WOMAN: No one else but we are.

UR'TAMROKOH: The gods will.

PO-JOE: We obey.

CHORUS:

Yan-ka-di

Ba-ba.

UR'TAMROKOH: The Oracle decides –

PO-JOE: We obey.

CHORUS:

Yan-ka-di oh

Yan-ka-di. Ba-ba.

UR'TAMROKOH:

T'nseecnh oh T'nseecnh oh

Krappo T'nseecnh oh.

T'nseecnh oh T'nseecnh oh

Krappo T'nseecnh oh.

ALL:

T'nseecnh oh T'nseecnh oh

Krappo T'nseecnh oh.

UR'TAMROKOH:

T'nseecnh oh T'nseecnh oh

Krappo T'nseecnh oh.

ALL:

T'nseecnh oh T'nseecnh oh.

(Gradually it begins to get dark. The transition is a slow one. In silhouette shadows pass to and fro on stage. People wander in and out. Gradually the stage is filled. Mask-like creatures performing masquerades: spirits of dead in white wrappers all cavort about. Some carry torches and lanterns made out of papier mache, carefully made and painted. Some look like houses in miniature; others like boats, ships, officers; Heads of State; politicians etc. Ur'Tamrokoh and the Women and Po-Joe all get swallowed up in the crowd. At first it is all calm and orderly. They chant as they move about on and off in different directions.)

CROWD *(dirge)*:

Hu. Hun. Hun. Hun *(Crowd swamp, some jumping and dancing.)*

Hun. Hun. Hun.

Walka-fas, walka-fas

Teda-nar-da, Walka-fas

Gee-me road, Gee-we road

Bad crowd da kam.

(It gets wilder. We see the four Gbakandas. They enter looking rough, tough and dancing jubilantly. The crowd gives way, but participate in a rather quiet movement rhythm.)

Gee we road. Gee we road

Bad crowd da kam.

Nar we dis. Nar we dis

Gbakanda crowd. Nar we dis. Gbakanda crowd

Shub leh we pass. Leh we pass

We da go. We want road

Gbakanda crowd.

Yetteh-teh

Yeti

Ye. Teh. Teh.

(The Beggar enters followed by the Shadow in silhouette. Their clothes dishevelled and they look worn out and beaten up.

They try to join in the dancing, but are pushed away. The Gbakandas get tough and real rough. They start dancing in circles. The Gbakanda Chorus Women enter led by Mammy-Queen. They clap their hands and do a rather soft and slow dance, clapping their hands to the right and then to the left. The dancing and singing get bigger and stronger. The Gbakandas dominating the show. Ur'Tamrokoh enters wearing a 'Ronko' with Umu at his side. She is dressed in a rich dyed satin-garra wrapper. They are followed behind by Po-Joe. The dancing stops when they enter. Everything goes silent.)

UR'TAMROKOH:

T'nseecnh oh T'nseecnh oh

Krappo T'jseench oh.

> *(The four Gbakandas surround Ur'Tamrokoh and Umu. They begin the Gbakanda dirge.)*

GBAKS:

Sie-Nandae

Ay-ay-ayaa

Sie-Nandae ohooooo

Sie-Nandae-ayaa

Sie-Nandae-ohooo

Tee-Gbengbeh ku-lorlee

1ST GBAK *(demanding Umu)*: Min nem ba-kor

UR'TAMROKOH *(touching him with his koboko)*: Ur'yeamo'ng.

(He falls face down.)

2ND GBAK:

Sie-Nandae

Ay-ay-ayaaaaaa

Sie-Nandae-Ohhhhhhh

Sie-Nandae

Ay-ay-ayaaaaaaaa

Sie-Nandae-ohoooooo

Tee-Gbengbeh

Ku-lorlee

(Affectionately to Umu.) Min nem ba-kor

UR'TAMROKOH (*hits the ground with his whip*): Ur'yeamo'ng. (*He goes down on his knees in supplication.*)

GBAKS:

Sie-Nandae
Ay-ay-ayaaaaa
Sie-Nandae-ohooooo
Sie-Nandae
Ay-ay-ay-aaaaaaa
Sie-Nandae-ohoooo
Tee-Gbengbeh ku-lorlee.

3RD GBAK (*genuflects and pleads*): Min nem ba'kor.

UR'TAMROKOH (*laughs scornfully and spits*): Ur'yeamo'ng. Min nem ba'kor.

GBAKS:

Sie-Nandae
Ay-ay-ay-aaaaaaaa
Sie-Nandae-ohhhhhhh
Sie-Nandae
Ay-ay-ayaaaaaaaaaa
Sie-Nandae-ohooooo
Tee-Gbengbeh ku-lorlee

4TH GBAK (*with a military determination and order*): Min nem ba'kor.

UR'TAMROKOH (*jumps up and grabs Umu wantonly. Stamps his feet hard and pulling her towards him very jealously*): Ur'yeamo'ng. Min nem ba'kor. Min nem ba'kor (*He sings.*)

Sie-Nandae
Ay-ay-ayaaaaaaaa
Sie-Nandae-ohhhhh
Sie-Nandae
Ay-ay-ayyaaaaaa
Sie-Nandae-ohooooo
Tee-Gbengbeh ku-lorlee. (*They walk slowly off stage.*)
Tee-Gbengbeh ku-lorlee. Tee-Gbengbeh ku-lorlee.
Tee-Gbengbeh ku-lorlee. Tee-Gbengbeh ku-lorlee.

(*The four Gbakandas pull each other up. The women and Po-Joe watch them. By this time the two drunks have gone out.*)

GBAKS (*they mournfully lament and walk away*):

Sie-Nandae
Ay-ay-ay-ay-aaaaaa
Sie-Nandae-ohooooo
Sie-Nandae
Ay-ay-ayaaaaaa
Tee-Gbengbeh ku-lorlee.

(*The Beggar, followed in silhouette by the Shadow, wanders on stage again and joins in the singing. They are finally left there by themselves singing: Tee-Gbengbeh ku-lorlee Tee-Gbengbeh ku-lorlee. Tee-Gbengbeh ku-lorlee.*)

BEGGAR (*realizing the loneliness*): There's no hope for the condemned.

SHADOW (*echoing voice, in silhouette*): Who are the condemned? They or us?

BEGGAR: Punny man. He is his own undoing. Try to help them and they'd have you stringed up a tree like Jim Crow. Blast, blast, blast.

SHADOW: So it is with you. When things don't go the way you expect and want; you begin to blast, blast, blast. We had better get going before those savages come looking to avenge us for the way we have embarrassed them.

BEGGAR: I don't understand it all. It is like a dream – a nightmare.

SHADOW: That's what life is. Few people can make it real like Ur'Tamrokoh. Let's go.

BEGGAR: That man Ur'Tamrokoh is corruption unsurpassed.

SHADOW: That is their way. They prefer it to be as it is. That's what they like, and want it to remain as it has been. Now let's quit before they get us as corrupt as they are. (*The voice echoes off singing. Silhouette of Shadow fades.*) Kan-kan-doma-doma Kan-kan-doma-doma. Kan-kan . . .

doma-doma. Kan-kan-doma-doma, Kan-kan, Doma-doma
Ur'Tamrokoh doma-doma. Umu-doma-doma. Gbakanda
doma-doma. (*He goes off.*)

BEGGAR: Wait. Wait for me. (*He walks about dazed.*) I don't
understand it all. I truly, honestly and sincerely don't
believe it could happen. Ur'Tamrokoh the corrupter. Umu
the disguised corrupt. Partners of evil deceits and exploits.
She was possessed by no devil. She was no sacrifice to any
god or Oracle. She's an actress of the greatest thieving
racket and plays her part well. What a good and clever
director, Ur'Tamrokoh is. A good seducer too. Old and
wise, schemish and simple. Umu, she knows how to lie
while her Gbakanda people love and lap the beauty of
untruths. She's a voluptuous maiden. I was jealous and
wanted her. We became cruel to Ur'Tamrokoh. To the
people of Gbakanda. No, we were not really; we spoke the
truth. (*Shouts.*) Did we? Did we? Umu she learned about
shame and made a Virtue of it. They torture her like an
animal, but she did not escape even when we insisted.
What was the use of our pleading for her to secede and get
her independence – for individual advantages – for what's
mine and what's not. She preferred to stay with them.
Her experience of suffering was only to strengthen her
will and make her indulge in it. For her, suffering is a way
to the truth. We were evil. We talked about fraternity and
humanitarianism. We were in the end the criminals. (*From
very near feet stamping and dancing and shouting and beating of
metal gadgets can be heard.*) Yes we were the criminals. We
talked of justice, when they, like kids, worshipped marble
stones – their longings, their wishful thoughts, they worship
them with tears of passion in their eyes; they pray to their
gods with voices ecclesiastical. Finally, their departing
joys were laughters echoed like children at play. (*The crowd
enters pushing and dancing wildly from every corner. Beggar
tries to get out but finds he is already trapped. He shouts.*) Let me
go! Let me out! Shadow. Shadow, where are you? The

light has played a trick on me. Shadow where are you?
Don't abandon me at this last minute. I am trapped like a
foolish fly in the spider's web. Help! Help! I am being
corrupted. Let me go, let me free. I am not of your kind.
Let me go. Let me go. (*His voice fades in the noisy crowd. For
music see p. 159.*)

CROWD (*jubilantly*):
  Yeti Yeh-teh-teh
  Yeti Yeh-ten-teh
  Bad crowd da kam
  Yeti-yeti . . . tet-teh-teh
  Umu-don-go
  Yeti Yeh-teh-yet-teh-teh.
  Gbakanda New Year
  Nar' im dis . . . Nar' im dis
  Shub-leh-we pass. Leh we go—Leh we go
  Gbakanda New Year. Ye-ti . . . yet-teh-teh—
  Move, move, easy.

Sie- na-ndae aye-ay- ayaa Sie- na-ndaeoo Sie-na-ndae aye- ay - ayaaa

Sie- na-ndaeoo Tee-gbe ng beh ku- lorlee

Go we must go doan d'wu meh

1. You beat me te-da Nar dar Gba naoh So fight fight so fight (So fight)Gba-kando Gbone
2. I'll kill you te- da nor body go know So fight fight so fight (So fight)Gba-kando Gbone

Drum
fight fight fight   to- morrow

Ritual Sneeze—the rhythm is the important thing

Repeat three times

Ti- so Ti- so Kra- ppo ti- so

I look I look I look I see my mother is co-ming If you have any gold

and sil-ver for me hang you must be hanged
save I must be saved

Rhythm

3 times

Ye- ti yeh-teh-teh Bad crowd da kam Nar'im dis Nar'im dis
Ye- ti yeh-teh-teh Umu-don-go
Ye- ti yeh-teh-teh Gba kanda New Year

Shub-leh-we pass leh we go leh we go Gba-ka-nda NewYear Ye ti yeh-teh-teh

move move easy

Yon-Kon

CHARACTERS

YON-KON
PAGU   } *Prisoners in the jail*
GBARATAE
OTHER PRISONERS
WARDER 99991
PRISON OFFICER
AGBA SAITEINY
SALU   } *Friends of Yon Kon*
BOBOR
AMADU

YON-KON

Men marching in a prison yard.

YON-KON (*shouting*): Right, left, left, right, right, left, left, right, right, left, left, right. Keep marching. Why do you stop?

PAGU: It's stupid! I'm tired.

YON-KON: Don't argue, keep marching. Right, left, left, right, right, left, left, right. Hey, hey, hey.

PAGU: We are not in the army. I can't do right, left, left, right. It's wrong.

YON-KON: In this prison yard you do as I say. If I, Yon-Kon, say right, left, left, right, then you march. (*Shouts.*) Right, left, left, right, right, left.

PAGU: You are just a prisoner like me, Yon-Kon. All of us here are prisoners.

(*Murmur from the marching Prisoners.*)

YON-KON: You are all different prisoners from me. I know everything about this prison yard. I have been here on and off since I was sixteen. I come in when I like, and I discharge when my time is over. (*Shouts.*) Right, left, left, right.

PAGU: That's all you know about here, right, left, left, right. I am not here for physical exercise. I have never been in prison before and I'm only here for two weeks.

YON-KON (*jovially*): We'll make it two weeks' hard labour, then. March! Right, left, left, right, right, left, left right.

PAGU: I am not taking any more orders from you, Yon-Kon.

YON-KON: No? Don't you be so sure. What's your name?

PAGU: I have no name.

YON-KON: Don't play tough with me, boy: you think because you are six-foot tall, big broad chest and hair like Samson, you are almighty? (*Laughs.*) Now, speak. (*Twisting his arm.*) Speak. What's your name?

(*Marching stops.*)

PAGU (*fights to free his arm*): Ai! You're breaking my arm. P-Pagu. My name is Pagu.

YON-KON: Pagu – is it? Well, now you are talking better, and clearly too. (*Laughs.*) You will answer some more questions.

PAGU: Let go my arm. I will tell you anything. Let go my arm.

YON-KON: No, I won't. You ask for it – rough. (*Laughs.*) I like it rough, with people like you who want to be tough.

PAGU: I was only joking.

YON-KON: Yah, joking eh? Tell me some more. (*Shouts.*) What's your name? Your full name?

PAGU (*groans*): Pagu Ekele.

YON-KON: Who is your mother?

PAGU: My mother is a trader. She is in Yaba, Nigeria – Ai! (*Prisoners laugh.*)

YON-KON: Who is your father?

PAGU: My father is a sailor. I don't know where he is. We've never met.

YON-KON: What is your profession?

PAGU: I was a store-keeper.

YON-KON: Where? Who for?

PAGU: At Kissy Town. For Ali Zasso, the Syrian merchant.

YON-KON: What is your nationality?

PAGU: I am of mixed blood. Half Krio, half Syrian.

YON-KON: Are you married?

PAGU: No!

YON-KON: How did you get involved with the police?

PAGU: Stealing. Oh, my arm. I stole a pair of shoes.

YON-KON: Is this your first offence?

PAGU: Yes! Yes!

YON-KON: Do you like it here? Would you like to come back? (*Pause.*) Answer!

PAGU (*yelps with pain*): Yes. No. No. Yes. (*Prisoners laugh.*)

YON-KON: You don't know. O.K. Now, we'll do some routine exercises, and marching.

PAGU (*groans*): Oh – Oh! You have blistered my arm.

YON-KON: You should be glad I dealt with you myself. If I had taken you to the quarter deck, you'd have had twelve lashes on your back, your hair shaved off your head, go around bare-footed, no meals, and sleep on a concrete floor, perhaps a wet one, for seven days.

PRISONER 1: You should thank Yon-Kon.

PRISONER 2: He is a good man.

PRISONER 3: He is boss around here.

PRISONER 4: Everybody respects him.

PRISONER 5: Everybody likes him.

PRISONER 6: Yeh – everybody likes him.

YON-KON: Up on your feet. Come on Pagu! Leave your arm alone. You over there, hey! Pa Gbaratae, come on. Attention!

(*They come to attention.*)

Routine exercises! After 'two'. You all know the words. One. Two.

PRISONERS:

We must not steal.
We must not steal.

We must not kill.
We must not kill.

We must not fight.
We must not fight.

We must not lie.
We must not lie.

We must obey the laws.
We must obey the laws.

We must behave
as good citizens should.

YON-KON: Right! Stand easy! (*They do.*)

Now, what are the things necessary to observe?

PRISONERS: Work hard, from Monday to Saturday, if
possible Sunday. Be responsible and respectable to yourself, your family, your neighbours. Pay your debts, and be
at enmity with no one. Be honest faithful, true and sincere
with yourself in whatever you do.

YON-KON: What do you promise to do when you leave here?

PRISONERS: The things we used to do that are wrong – we
will do them no more.

The places we used to go that are bad – we will go there
no more.

The words we used to curse and swear – we will use them
no more.

(*Prison clock strikes twelve.*)

YON-KON: O.K. Good. It's twelve o'clock, time for lunch.
Attention!

(*They come to attention.*)

Quick march! Ready – go!

(*They march.*)

Right, left, left, right, right, left, left, right.

PRISONERS: We will be good. We will be good. We will be
good.

(*Marching and Prisoners going.*)

YON-KON: Pa Gbaratae, keep my chair for me. I want to
send a quick message.

PRISONERS (*chant in distance*): We will be good. We will be
good.

(*Yon-Kon takes receiver up from hook, dials three numbers.*)

YON-KON: Is that the Orderly Room? Er – let me speak to
Warder nine-nine-double-nine-one. (*Pause – laughs.*) Ah!
It's me, Yon-Kon, Chief Prisoner. Ah! Nine-nine-double-
nine-one: what's cooking? Yeh! Well, I got me a new
recruit today. He was being a little roughy-toughy . . .

but . . . eh, I handled him kinda well . . . yea. He knows me now. Well and proper too. But – eh, that's not what I wanted to talk to you about. I am just going for my lunch. You know I discharge tomorrow; yeh, well, I want you to take a message for me to Agba. You know, Agba Saiteiny. Tell him to send a taxi to collect me tomorrow morning at 6.30 a.m. Yes, I want to travel in style. I want to leave this yard and forget all about it tomorrow. In and out of this Pademba prison for forty years is enough for me. I mean it! When I leave here tomorrow I will never come back. Not as a prisoner, anyway. (*Laughs.*) Tell Agba that . . . and tell him to come with the taxi himself. Tell him not to be late. O.K. Bye.

SCENE TWO

The Prison Canteen

GBARATAE (*angry*): I tell you, Pagu, don't sit on that chair.

PAGU: Why not? I will eat my dinner where I like. And I like this chair.

PRISONER 1: You looking for more trouble?

PRISONER 2: Ay! You going to get it tough with Yon-Kon.

PRISONER 3: You look out for Yon-Kon.

PRISONER 4: He won't like this.

PAGU: Why the hell are you all afraid of Yon-Kon? He's not a god.

PRISONER 1: I am not afraid of Yon-Kon.

PRISONER 2: I am not scared of no-one.

PRISONER 3: But Yon-Kon is the boss.

PAGU: Oh, yes. You're all frightened of him. You all worship him – as if he's a blasted . . .

GBARATAE: Get off that chair. (*They scuffle.*) I warned you, Pagu. Little upstart. (*Slap.*) Untrained! (*Slap.*) Uncultured! (*Slap.*)

(*Laughter and murmurs of encouragement from prisoners.*)
I'll give you the training your silly lazy mother didn't give
you.

PAGU (*losing his temper*): You keep your filthy tongue off my
mother. You . . . you . . .

(*Struggle. Prisoners encourage fight which ends in Pagu
smashing chair over Gbaratae's head. He falls to the ground.*)

PRISONER 1: Pagu, get away from Pa Gbaratae.

PRISONER 2: You will kill the old man.

PRISONER 3: Separate them.

PRISONER 4: Help Pa Gbaratae up.

PRISONER 5: Yon-Kon, Yon-Kon, come quickly!

YON-KON (*coming*): What's going on? (*Approaches.*) Who's
that on the floor?

PAGU: I didn't mean it, Yon-Kon. He abused my mother.
He wouldn't let me sit on the chair. He hit me. I was only
defending myself.

YON-KON: You break a man's head with a chair, and you
claim it's self-defence. What are you all standing gaping
at? Ring the alarm bell, call the Governor, get the doctor.
Pagu, get some water.

(*Alarm bell.*)

99991 (*approaching*): What's been going on here, Yon-Kon?

YON-KON: I was not here, Sir, I was on the telephone.

PAGU (*returns*): Here is the water, Yon-Kon.

YON-KON: We don't need water – he is dead.

(*Bowl of water drops.*)

PAGU: Dead? Dead? But how could he be?

99991: No – no. He's not dead, he's still breathing. Get
some prisoners to take him to the hospital. You come with
me to the Governor's office, Pagu.

PAGU: I didn't mean it. I didn't mean it. He abused my
mother. Abused her.

SCENE THREE

Agba Saiteiny's. Evening – the same day. Drum music, singing, shouting. For music see p. 183.

SALU (*singing*):
Sarah-ayaaaaaa
sarah-sarah-muna-yaah
sarah, fine, fine sarah
sarah, minnie, minnie sarah
when a 'member duah-la
sarah-muna-yah.
O ti-na-na-na-na, ti na-nazo
ti-na-na-na, ti na-na, motor driver
I don't care.

AGBA: Stop! (*Shouts.*) Stop! We must finish sharing last night's business before Gumbay practice.

SALU (*swell of music and singing*):
. . . oba . . . ah-ya
go-da
ge-am; take-am;
put-am; pull-am; shake-am . . . ah . . . yaaaaaa

AGBA: Stop! (*Music subsides.*) O.K. O.K. All you boys done good job last night. Here, Salu, you take this, plenty good, good lappa for you wive and mother.

SALU: I no like lappa. I want that cotton bale.

AGBA: Take what I give you! Right?

SALU: O.K. Right! No argue with you, Agba, you are big boss of the Gumbay – but remember, this night we got big job to do.

AGBA: Bobor, you take this clock. Plenty money when you sell it.

BOBOR: Yes, Agba. I fit sell it for my neighbour.

AGBA: Amadu, you take the cotton bale.
(*Hard knocking on front door.*)
Put all the stuff in that room. Bolt the door. Quick, now.

Bobor, Amadu, crack the Gumbay while we hide this other stuff. (*They beat the Gumbay Drums venomously as the knocking increases non-stop, and singing as well. For music see p. 184.*)

SALU (*sings*):

Ma ma-aya, mama-aya-ma
pingila
I don't play with boys ma
I never steal ma
pingila
I never swear ma
pingila
Ma-ma forgive me
pingila
Ma-ma, forgive me
pingila.

99991 (*from outside*): Agba Saiteiny – is Agba Saiteiny home?

AGBA (*going*): Coming. Coming – don't break the door down.

99991 (*from outside*): Agba, good you are home.

AGBA: Don't beat on me door like that. This is not the prison gate. (*Door opens.*)
Oh! What brings you here, nine-nine-double-nine-one? Stop the Gumbay, boys. It's a visitor. From the prison. (*Gumbay stops.*)

99991: You always pull a long face on me, Agba. Why?

AGBA: Uniform men and me don't get on.

99991: Why?

AGBA: I got work to do. You got any message for me? Out with it.

99991: Are you not going to ask me in?

AGBA: For what? When next I come to prison, deal with me accordingly.

99991: It is a long time since you have not been in.

AGBA: Is that why you come to visit me?

99991: No, no. I have a message from Yon-Kon. He is

discharged tomorrow. He wants you to meet him – the usual time – 6.30 a.m. He says you should come and pick him up with a taxi, because he is not going to cross the prison gates any more. Not as a prisoner anyway.

AGBA: Is that all? Goodbye. (*Door slams.*) You hear that? Yon-Kon is coming out in the morning. Salu, go and rent a taxi. No night-business tonight. We must be in good condition in the morning. Fit. Amadu, Bobor, you clean the house. I will go and buy some nick-nacks and Agbakra. (*Laughs.*) The Gumbay will be just right for any engagement now – and Christmas just round the corner! Boy, boy, boy. We will swing, left right and centre. Without Yon-Kon the group is not complete. (*Gaily.*) We need him, we want him, everyone misses him when he's away.

SALU: I hope this time he will stay away from stealing fowls.

AGBA: I will talk to him tomorrow. Give me me hat, Salu, I am going to buy the nick-nacks.

SCENE FOUR

Prison cell, the wall-clock is ticking.

PAGU (*to himself*): I don't like the way that clock ticks. (*Shouts.*) Quiet! Be quiet! (*Pause.*) Yon-Kon . . . Yon-Kon. Mr Yon-Kon, are you there? Can you hear me? Get me out of this cell. Yon-Kon, Mr Yon-Kon.
    (*Cell door unlocked and opened.*)

YON-KON: Why are you screaming?

PAGU: Is he dead, Yon-Kon? What did the doctor say? Are they going to hang me? Can't you help me?

YON-KON: How can I help you? I am just a prisoner like you.

PAGU: But you are a different prisoner. You said so.

YON-KON: That is true. But not in a situation like this.
    (*Pause.*)

PAGU: Listen to that clock. It is driving me mad.

YON-KON: Well, don't listen to it.

PAGU: I feel as if I am in a condemned cell. It is so damp. There is no bed. How long will they keep me here?

YON-KON (*going*): I don't know.

PAGU: Don't go, Yon-Kon. Stay with me.

YON-KON: I have to pack. I discharge in the morning.

PAGU: Please stay.

YON-KON: Whether I stay or not makes no difference.

PAGU: It was self-defence. I haven't the mind to kill a fly.

YON-KON: Don't try to convince me, Pagu. Keep your pleas for the judge and jury. They will understand you better.

PAGU: You are hard; you don't want to help me. You don't want to understand.

YON-KON: Prison life, Pagu, is a different life. A different world with strange stories. You never know what to understand or who to help.

PAGU: What do you mean?

YON-KON: The understanding and help you want should have come from your home, or your friends.

PAGU: But I have no friends. Those who helped me spend my money deserted me when I was in trouble.

YON-KON: You see: that's the secret. Everything you do with your life must be well planned and well done. The laws are made by man, for man to observe and obey. The moment you slip, you are in the net.

PAGU: How old are you, Yon-Kon?

YON-KON: Fifty six.

PAGU: How long have you been in prison?

YON-KON (*laughs*): This time, nine months. But I have been in and out of this prison for forty years. I got my first lock-up when I was sixteen.

PAGU: What did you do?

YON-KON (*imitates cock crowing*): I stole a cock.

PAGU: A cock – why?

YON-KON: I like playing with them. The way people play with dogs and cats.

PAGU: Do you always get sent to prison for stealing cocks?

YON-KON: Yep.

PAGU: Why not rob a bank or something valuable?

YON-KON: I don't believe in robbing banks – and I don't steal fowls to sell them. No! You see, when I was a child I spent all my time with fowls, breeding them, sleeping with them.

PAGU: You can't sleep with fowls.

YON-KON: Oh yes, I slept in the barn where the fowls were.

PAGU: Why did your parents allow you to?

YON-KON: Oh, it wasn't my parents. I lived with a foster-mother. My father died before I was born and my mother two days after.

PAGU: I'm sorry.

YON-KON: Sorry! For what? Yes, I used to take care of those fowls, and they knew me like any dog or cat knows its master! The cocks used to wake me up in the morning. (*Imitates crowing.*) Ko-ko-ri-oh-ko-urrr. (*Laughs.*) Six o' clock – to the dot. The hens and chickens – chi-chi-chik – used to follow me about for their rice and corn. I never let them into the streets. One day, I killed a dog that frightened them and my foster-mother was so angry, she turned me out of the house. I tried to get a job. (*Laughs.*) It was impossible. I had no education or technical skill.

PAGU: But you . . .

YON-KON: Don't interrupt! I like fowls. I always wanted to collect them, and seeing them straying about in the streets makes me angry, because they easily get killed. The first fowl I took I didn't mean to steal, I thought it was a stray.

PAGU: And that was how you got your first lock-up?

YON-KON: Yah, and so it goes on – especially around Christmas. I pick up a fowl, get arrested, judged, and sent in for six or nine months every year, and for the past forty years, I've always spent my Christmas in here.

PAGU: And you like it here?

YON-KON: I like it the way I do it. Half of the year am out, the other half am in here, resting.

PAGU: Resting?

YON-KON: Yah, resting. I have to rest, and I can rest better in here because I am so at home here. I am happy in most ways. But I'd hate to spend six or seven years in here at a stretch.

PAGU: I will never get out of here any more. (*Cries.*) I am a criminal, a murderer.

YON-KON: No, you are not! But you shouldn't have lost your temper, you know. Gbaratae did not die on the spot.

PAGU (*eagerly*): No?

YON-KON: They'll charge you with manslaughter, I expect. If the other prisoners like you, they will speak up for you.

PAGU: Yon-Kon, help me. Get them to tell the truth. He slapped me, humiliated me, abused my mother.

YON-KON: And you didn't like that?

PAGU: No one who abuses my mother gets away with it.

YON-KON: I am a bit puzzled.

PAGU: About what?

YON-KON: The doctor.

PAGU: Why?

YON-KON: How much have you got in the bank?

PAGU: Why?

YON-KON (*shouts*): I want to help you. How much have you got in the bank?

PAGU: Not much. Only . . . Well . . .

YON-KON: Speak up, boy! How many figures? Two, three, four?

PAGU: Two . . . Two hundred and something, I can't remember. My bank book is with my mother.

YON-KON: Not bad. Is your mother well off?

PAGU: How do you mean?

YON-KON: Has she got money? Would she help you?

PAGU: Leave my mother out of this. If you want to help me, you can, without asking about my mother and my savings.

Can't we help each other out of human kindness and sympathy? I didn't kill Gbaratae because I hated him. I was trying to defend myself. I am not a murderer.

YON-KON: You are a coward, you are frightened. Ever since you started bragging this morning, I knew the kind of boy you are. I was like you.

PAGU: I'm not like you.

YON-KON: I was like you.

PAGU (*shouts*): I'm not like you.
    (*Thunder with rain later.*)

YON-KON: Ya, thunder. It is a sign. (*Laughs*) Yah, I was like you, Pagu, years ago. I was like you when I first come to prison – talk, brag, fight.

PAGU: I'm not like you. No two people are the same. And you didn't kill a man the first time you were here.

YON-KON: No! I didn't kill a man, but I stabbed three men – two prisoners and a warder.

PAGU: Did they die?

YON-KON: No, they survived. With indelible scars.

PAGU: Why did you stab them?

YON-KON: They hurt my pride.

PAGU: What did they do to you? I mean the Law?

YON-KON (*laughs*): Nothing. I got away with it by spending the last penny I had. 'See to see', boy, '*See* to *see*'.

PAGU (*puzzled*): I see.

YON-KON: Can you hear the rain? It is full moon tomorrow, and I'll be out of here. It is late now, I must go. You don't need my help? Do you?

PAGU: No! Not that way.

YON-KON: I am only advising you. You can take it or leave it. I can see doctor and talk to him – he is a good man. That is, if you'll spend your two hundred pounds, of course.

PAGU: How can my two hundred pounds save me?

YON-KON: That's easy, Pagu. Doc is a clever man. One: as I see it, Gbaratae was a dying man. He always had stroke and heart trouble. Two: you were trying to defend yourself, and under great emotional strain and the balance of your mind was disturbed, due to reasons which Doc can analyze. Three: Gbaratae, according to Doc, was alive when we took him to the hospital. He died fifteen minutes later . . . um . . . from the fracture Gbaratae had on his skull, it is obvious it wasn't a blow inflicted by you, from you, or any object handled by you.

PAGU: Then who inflicted that blow?

YON-KON: The pavement, man. He had a stroke. He fell and hit his skull on the pavement.

PAGU: So that is your defence for me. What about the prisoners?

YON-KON: They didn't see you hit him!

PAGU: They didn't? Do you expect me to believe you can arrange all this? So I can give you my life savings to get me free?

YON-KON: Oh no! You don't have to believe me or give me the money either. As I said earlier, it's just an advice. Take it or leave it. But think about it, and remember, there are times when we pay for our innocence. It's not too dear a price.

PAGU: Listen, Yon-Kon. I come from a good home. I don't believe in bribery, deceit or injustice. I'd rather die. I asked you to help me, because you're an older man with much more experience, prison experience. Why should I bribe you or anyone else? I know I'm not guilty.

YON-KON: You've got a lot to learn.

PAGU: Not from you, Yon-Kon. Not what you are trying to sell me.

YON-KON: Many years ago, I thought the same thing. I felt the same way. (*Starts acting the past cat-calls people usually associate him with.*) But my pride was killed when people called me 'Jail bird' – and children sang 'Yon-Kon pass me dollar loss, Yon-Kon pass me dollar go'. They beat tin pans behind me singing, 'Tiffy tiffy, jan-kon-ni-ko 'e tif fowl, jan-kon-ni-ko, white cock, jan-kon-ni-ko'. (*Laughs.*) Yes, that was a long time ago. (*Sighs.*) Well, the rain's stopped. Goodnight. But think of my advice and forget your pride. A prisoner hasn't got any. (*Going.*) And stop being a coward.

(*Cell door closed and locked.*)

SCENE FIVE

Agba's new place; it is about six months later. Frogs croaking and evening birds singing.

99991 (*off, calling*): Agba . . . Agba . . . Agba Saiteiny!

AGBA: You want to talk to me warder, come over here!

99991: Hello, Agba!

AGBA: Hi!

99991: I have been looking for Yon-Kon for over three weeks I didn't know you'd moved from your old house.

AGBA: Ah, we moved six months ago.

99991: Why?

AGBA: People complain we make too much noise with the Gumbay drums.

99991: How is Yon-Kon? He seems to be keeping his promise.

AGBA: Yon-Kon is not changed, nine-nine-double-nine-one, he still steals fowls. Lucky for us they don't catch him.

99991: But he –

AGBA: The other day he nearly got into trouble. That's why we move up the hill.

99991: He promised not to steal fowls any more.

AGBA: He will never stop. I can't stop him. You can't stop him. Nobody can. He's made that way.

99991: Where is he now?

AGBA: We have small palava, small quarrel. I don't know where he is.

99991: I have a message for him, from Pagu.

AGBA: Maybe he will come back soon.

99991: I thought you were good friends and were getting on well with the Gumbay business.

AGBA: Yon-Kon don't like it here with me again. He don't want any more to do with the Gumbay. He say we idle, lazy and free. But that is all I can do – Gumbay is my life.

99991: I must go now, am going on duty.

AGBA: What is the message?

99991: Oh, yes. Well, you know about that Pagu Ekele – sentenced to seven years imprisonment for manslaughter, while he was serving two weeks hard labour for shoe-stealing.

AGBA: Oh, yes.

99991: Well, his mother died some months ago in a road accident. Since then he has been sort of going out of his head . . . mad . . .

AGBA: Poor thing.

99991: He's in hospital very ill, not eating, talks to no one. Three weeks ago he asked me to tell Yon-Kon he wants to see him – I think he wants to tell him something. So if Yon-Kon could come to the prison tomorrow morning . . . I think Pagu needs his help greatly.

AGBA: I will tell him tonight when he comes back.

99991: Well, goodbye, Agba! Thank heavens you don't pull a long face at me any more.

AGBA: There is a time for everything, nine-nine-double-nine-one. A time for everything.

SCENE SIX

Agba's old place.

AGBA: Bobor. Salu. Amadu. Yon-Kon. Anyone home?

YON-KON: Ai.

AGBA: When did you come back, Yon-Kon?

YON-KON: Can't remember, but am kicking out again.

AGBA: This evening? Now?

YON-KON: Yah.

AGBA: Where to?

YON-KON: Prison maybe.

AGBA: Prison? Are you out of your mind?

YON-KON: Ha! You think I am?

AGBA: If the only place you think about is prison, there must be something wrong with you.

YON-KON: There are many things wrong with me. For a start, I am not happy here with you and your Gumbay set.

AGBA: That's no reason why you should be proud of going back to prison.

YON-KON: It is the only place I can be proud of. I feel happy and content there.

AGBA: But you promised not to go there again.

YON-KON: I did! Nine months ago. That's a long time now, and what have I got being out of jail? No friends, no job, no nothing. In prison I enjoy the jollof-rice, ginger beer, cakes, band entertainments, important visitors, discussions and many other things.

AGBA: I use to enjoy all those things too. We both use to. And we can enjoy them still better outside, where we are free.

YON-KON: I don't feel free outside. I'll never feel free or enjoy anything outside prison. Prison was built for people like me.

AGBA: No, Yon-Kon, that is not true.

YON-KON: For me it is true. I'll always make new friends there. I will have people to command. It is the only life I understand, and the place I know best.

    (*Pause.*)

AGBA: Nine-nine-double-nine-one was here to see you.

YON-KON: Yes! He still remembers me. I know they miss me. Warders as well as prisoners.

AGBA: They don't miss you! They respect you. They respect you because they think you are keeping your promise.

YON-KON: Ha! Promise? Well, they will soon welcome me in again. Maybe tomorrow.

AGBA: Yon-Kon, you are not going –

YON-KON: Yes, I am. I go in when I like, when I want to . . . Christmas is just round the corner – I mustn't miss a Christmas in prison.

AGBA: I've a message for you.

YON-KON: Who from?

AGBA: Pagu! Nine-nine-double-nine-one says that he wants to see you very much.

YON-KON: For what? He never took my advice – he was too big-manish, too proud, too good to listen to me.

AGBA: Don't you think you are like that?

YON-KON (*laughs scornfully*): You're kidding. I'm not.

AGBA: If you knew yourself, you wouldn't be so sure. Anyway, according to nine-nine-double-nine-one, Pagu's mother is dead, killed in a road accident, and he is very ill, going mad, not eating, talks to no-one.

YON-KON: You see, they need me. Well, when I get in, he'll do routine exercises for me, sick or well. Sane or insane.

AGBA: You bet he will.

YON-KON: Go find me a taxi. I am going to confess my crimes and get back to prison. (*Breaks into song. Self-made words and tune.*) Krismes da kam, I mus' go back to prison, pick-up a chicken and get sent in for six months oh, ya, happy krismes me nor die oh, merry krismes me nor die ay.

(*He beats on the Gumbay Drums.*)

krismes is krismes, no matter where you spend it,

krismes is for we all, so long as we are happy.

Happy krismes me nor die ohooo

Merry krismes me nor die ayaaaaa

SCENE SEVEN

The Warder's Office

99991: Who've you got for us today, constable?

OFFICER: Only one prisoner, sir. Yon-Kon.

99991: What? Well, Yon-Kon, you have not kept your promise then?

YON-KON: No, sir. You see.

99991: Fowl stealing again, eh?

YON-KON: Yes, sir. You see I found I couldn't be happy.

99991: Take him to his usual block. Oh, yes, we kept it for you. We thought you might come back some day.

YON-KON: Thank you, Sir. How are things, eh? Still the same routine?

99991: Still the same.

YON-KON: And the prisoners? How are they making out? How is – eh – Pagu?

99991: All right, Yon-Kon, you go and find out. They're all yours again. You are back in charge.

SCENE EIGHT

Prison yard.

YON-KON: Right, left, left, right, right, left, left, right, right, left, left, right, right, left. Pagu, Pagu, come here.

PAGU (*approaches*): Yon-Kon. Yon-Kon, I want to talk to you.

YON-KON: For the past three weeks, I hear you've been dodging routine exercises, why?

PAGU: On doctor's orders. I must.

YON-KON: Join the rank. Doctor's orders or not – fall in line.

PAGU: But, Yon-Kon. I . . . I . . .

YON-KON: Yap, yap, yap. Don't argue.

PAGU: Yon-Kon, I must talk to you. It's urgent. It is very important.

YON-KON: Later.

PAGU: Did you know my mother is dead? Did you get my message?

YON-KON: I did. Now fall into line. Right, left, left right.

PAGU: I wasn't there to give my mother a burial. I don't know what's happened to my money – she had everything – every penny.

YON-KON: We'll talk about everything later. There is plenty

of time. (*Shouts.*) Right, left, left, right. (*To Pagu.*) Don't
stand there gaping and wailing, Pagu! Fall into line . . .

PAGU: I . . . I . . .

YON-KON: Yap, yap, yap! Don't argue. You are wasting
my time. Halt!

    (*They do.*)

Now, you prisoners, routine exercises. Come on, Pagu.
Hey! You over there, come on. After two – You all know
the words. One, two.

PRISONERS:

  We must not steal
  We must not steal

  We must not kill
  We must not kill

  We must not fight
  We must not fight

  We must not lie
  We must not lie

  We must obey the laws
  We must obey the laws

  We must behave
  As good citizens should.

YON-KON: That right. Now, quick march. Ready, go!

    (*Marching.*)

Left, right, right, left, left, right, right, left, left, right, right,
left.